AWAKEN

HEART

OF THE BELOVED

COMMUNITY

AUDRI SCOTT WILLIAMS

FORWARD BY
AMELIA PLATTS BOYNTON ROBINSON

COVER ART BY
Karen Hunter Watson

Printed in the United States of America

Second Edition, 2015

ISBN 978-0-9670239-5-3

NOWTIME Publishing
P.O. Box 126
Cottonwood, Alabama 36320
Web: www.belovedcommunityawakening.com
Email: aew.bcawakening@gmail.com

Front cover artwork by Karen Hunter Watson
Back cover photo by Victoria Scott

Book design and layout by Mikuak Rai

DEDICATION

There isn't any way I can usher you into the beloved community you will find here in these pages without recognizing a very special iconic woman who continually grounds me in my sense of purpose, and who reminds me of the importance of walking my path, regardless of whether or not it appears that I am making a difference.

As she says, "…just keep on walking and spreading seeds of love because, whether it is in your life time or not, one day they will sprout and change the world, even if it takes 200 years, just keep on keeping on."

Mrs. Amelia Platts Boynton Robinson, the Matriarch of the Voting Rights Bill, and one of the organizers of what came to be known as "Bloody Sunday" (the first attempt at the Selma to Montgomery bridge crossing on March 7, 1965 – exactly 50 years ago today), was violently attacked as she and over six hundred walkers attempted the crossing. The brutality she and fellow marchers (17 had to be hospitalized) endured would be captured in photographs and video to become one of the definitive moments that turned the tide in the Civil and Voting Rights movements.

At 103 years wise, she continues to share her wisdom with anyone who is willing and ready to listen. I can still hear her saying, "Don't stand on my shoulders. Get out there and make your mark."

And, I might add, "Every generation has its own bridges to cross!"

I dedicate *Awakening the Heart of the Beloved Community* to Mrs. Amelia Platts Boynton Robinson and all of those who are willing to live into their passion for peace and justice with a commitment to seeing the world through the eyes of all the "others" that remind us of who we can become – together!

Audri Scott Williams – March 7, 2015

ACKNOWLEDGEMENTS

It has taken a village to raise this "child" – *Awakening the Heart of the Beloved Community*. There are so many beautiful souls who refused to let "life" get in the way of the publishing of *Awakening the Heart of the Beloved Community*. To all of you, thank you for your love and support, your kind and encouraging words, and your prayers.

You cleared the road and made me believe in my own possibilities. I pray this book does the same for others.

Specifically, I want to thank Karen Hunter Watson, my partner and co-founder of the Quantum Leap Transformational Center, cover artist and co-producer of the companion *Awakening* musical CD, and fellow global peace walker - thank you for constantly reminding me to breath and trust, and holding my feet to the fire when I was having one of my moments!

Thank you to the best Papa in the whole world, Mr. Henry Jones -- Papa to all of his favorite daughters.

Baba Ojiji, Dr. Richard Puls, for believing in the Grandmothers and their wisdom, and for believing in me to carry out their directives.

To all of the authors who found their way here, welcome home. Thank you for your trust.

To everyone who showed up at the Quantum Leap Transformation Center for one purpose only; to realize you were called here to lend a service to the work at hand.

Thank you for rolling up your sleeves and getting to work editing, transcribing, and generating ideas for getting the word out. Thank you Janet WindWalker Jones, Victoria Scott, Angie Blackwell, Tori Wolfe-Sisson, and Shante Wolfe-Sisson.

Thank you Lenett Neffaahtiti Partlow-Myrick and Mikuak Rai for your long hours of editing. Thank you again, Mikuak Rai, for co-producing the companion musical CD, *Awakening*, and for standing in to serve as publicist to help get the word out about the book!! Many thank yous to my SEC Dothan spiritual community -- your prayers are powerful!!

And to my beloved community, you make me strong and open my eyes to the power we have, together, to change the world!

Table of Contents

FORWARD..i

PREFACE...v

INTRODUCTION...ix

Part One: THE AWAKENING..........................1
We Are Now Co-Creating The Future...................3
Love: The Ultimate Peacemaker.........................7

Part Two: THE ARTS...................................11
The Arts And Our Beloved Community................13

My Beloved Community................................17

Storytelling: How It Helps Build The Beloved
Community...21
Story Bridge...25
The Inheritance Of The Hip Hop Generation..........31

Luck...39

Unplugged...43

Part Three: PERSONAL &
COMMUNITY HEALTH...............................47
Psychological Preparedness:

What Do We Teach Our Youth?........................49

The Beloved Community:

A Mental Health Perspective...........................55

Growing Up On The West Side Of Baltimore.........59

The Scent Of A Place...................................65

Why Therapy On A Farm?

The Journey To Jenlo Farm.............................73

Part Four: JUSTICE..**77**
　Restorative Justice..79

　The Responsibility Of Leadership........................83
　Leonard Peltier..89
　What Good Is Talking Nobody's Listening?.................93
Part Five: HONORING DIFFERENCE..............**105**
　I AM...107
　When Disability Is The Difference
　And The Beloved Community............................121
　Vision Of A World That Works For All.................125
　A College Teacher's Experience Of
　Beloved Community..133
　Indigenous Call For Urgent, Unprecedented, And
　Unified Action For Protecting And Restoring The
　Sacred..137
Part Six: INTERFAITH
　Interfaith In The Deep South...........................145
　Love, Compassion, Empathy, And
　Peacebuilding..149
　What Mother Mary Means To Me.....................153
　The Third Fire..159
CONCLUSION..**173**
ABOUT THE AUTHOR...............................**175**

FORWARD

By Amelia Platts Boynton Robinson
Matriarch of the Voting Rights Movement

Dear Audri:

This letter is to confirm my confidence and trust in you. You are an extraordinary human being, who is undoubtedly committed to love, peace, and justice for the people of this world.

Whereas, some people talk about love and peace, but never take any meaningful actions to bring it about, and some others measure their pursuit for peace in communities in terms of bullets and bombs, you have demonstrated a belief that prayer, love, meaningful communications, and human sharing will best bring real peace and justice in the world.

In addition, you and your team's 3½ year walk around the world, among your other humane adventures spewing vibes of love and peace every step of the way, clearly indicated that you possess the right stuff to carry on whenever and wherever I leave off, making it pleasing and proper for me – as your senior – to "pass my freedom, peace, and justice torch" to you, and charging you with a perpetual pursuit of freedom, peace, and justice for as long as God blesses you with the health and spirit to do so.

Please continue to treasure the fact that our children are 100% our future and must be treated accordingly. Good education and quality examples set by adults will undoubtedly serve as their best guides to survival and success.

Your vision, courage, and commitment to making this world a more peaceful place for all is absolutely commendable.

Sincerely,
Amelia Platts Boynton Robinson
Matriarch of the Voting Rights Movement

Mrs. Amelia Platts Boynton Robinson, at 103 years old, has stood for "right" all of her life. Born in Savannah, Georgia in 1911, her civil rights activities began at age nine, as she traveled by horse and buggy with her mother, Anna Eliza Hicks, teaching colored people to register and vote in the 1920s. She moved to Selma and registered to vote in 1932. She and her first husband, Samuel W. Boynton, dedicated their lives to public service by fighting to enhance the quality of life for Black Americans. They were discriminated against by Whites, and ostracized by many Blacks. Mr. Boynton was driven to an early death; and, Mrs. Boynton was falsely arrested on the streets of Selma by Dallas County Sheriff Jim Clark. Moreover, she was beaten-down on the Edmund Pettus Bridge on March 7, 1965 (Bloody Sunday), by Alabama state troopers and other lawmen. Her differences with law enforcement were reconciled in 2007.

Her monument stands at the foot of the bridge thanks to the National Southern Christian Leadership Conference Women's Organization, alongside U. S. Congressman, John Lewis, and Civil Rights Icon, Hosea Williams. She visited Germany, Italy, Bahamas, as well as many American cities inspiring young people to stand-up for their civil and human rights. Her awards and honors are too numerous to mention. She is a writer, historian and publisher. Mrs. Robinson dreams of a Village of Hope, designed to identify and save our children from themselves first, and everything else next.

PREFACE
Audri Scott Williams

Awakening the Heart of the Beloved Community, as you will experience it here, is far from my original idea for the book. Initially, I was caught up in the "rapture" of the promises of the "beloved community" that I heard over and over again as a child of the civil rights era.

I was held captive in Dr. Martin Luther King's Christian theologically based "promised land" where the beloved community resides. The sound bites from his speeches during the late 1950s and 1960s still ring in my ears and in my heart. This is where I began.

So I began enthusiastically, and armed with a great title: The Heart of the Beloved Community, The Courage to Love. Then something happened - I call it my reality check. Everywhere I turned to look at the beloved community, I found groups that I once thought of as the example of the beloved community to be groups of like-minded and spirited people doing a great work together. This sounds good, right?

But as I began looking through the lens of the core elements of the beloved community, they did not measure up. Most obvious indicators of the lack of inclusivity were: racial and ethnic grouping, faith-based circles that did not engage other faiths nor different spiritual practices; similar economic and educational attainment; few had LGBTQ representation; and there was a lack of multi-generational participation.

In frustration, I was led to change the working title of the book to In Search of the Beloved Community. The consequence of this was an unsettled perception that we have not come very far. Sure, since the 90's, laws have changed and desegregation is no longer an issue – or is it? – And the journey began anew.

In this state of awareness, everything in me screamed, "Do not abandon the search, you are almost there. Make the book the model of inclusion. Allow the diverse voices from diverse paths to merge between the pages, engaging the reader in their own safe space."

Then it dawned on me that the book is about feeding the great awakening that is happening in so many areas of our society, culture, and traditional and nontraditional faith based choices.

I realized that the most productive thing I could do was to amass the beloved community between the pages of the book. Give voice to as broad a spectrum of the population as possible (in the United States primarily, with an international version to follow). The next challenge was to allow the reader to become the "deep listener", as they journeyed through the chapters as though creating a great tapestry or quilt. Using my story as the stitching and binding elements to bring the pieces together stronger and richer than any one piece could ever be, I set out on a new mission - to awaken the heart of the beloved community.

Now the book in me had a name and a place and a VOICE. *Awakening the Heart of the Beloved Community* honors the collective tensions, as well as the collective opportunity for transformation. Transformation to what? - as Shariff Abdullah says, in chapter 21, - a world that works for all.

INTRODUCTION

Nearly a century ago, my definition of the Beloved Community would be centered around the works and words of 20th century philosopher, Josiah Royce, founder of the Fellowship of Reconciliation.

Josiah Royce coined the term, Beloved Community, recognizing that each person has a dual purpose - to serve themselves as an individual, and to serve their community. The stage was set for us to embrace individualism - being independent and self-reliant while in service to the greater good through the Beloved Community. He identified two elements that are essential to the creation and sustainability of the Beloved Community: loyalty and Agape love. Agape love suggests that we are to love others sacrificially. In Christian theology, *Jesus gave the parable of the Good Samaritan as an example of sacrifice for the sake of others, even for those who may care nothing at all for us, or even hate us, as the Jews did the Samaritans. Sacrificial love is not based on a feeling, but a determined act of the will, a joyful resolve to put the welfare of others above our own.*

He says, "…choose your cause and then serve it…My life means nothing, either theoretically or practically, unless I am a member of a community." (Royce 2001 [1913] 357)

Nearly fifty years later Dr. Martin Luther King, Jr. popularized the concept of the Beloved Community as a form of social action to transform the injustices of racism and poverty. He often said that the end was "the creation of the Beloved Community." This he saw as the community of brotherly/sisterly love capable of birthing heaven on earth. At the core of King's idea of the Beloved Community was also Agape love that had its origins in the Christian story of the Good Samaritan.

Reverend Dr. Martin Luther King, Jr. embed the concept of the Beloved Community into the consciousness of America and the world during the struggle for civil rights in the South…a new social order! He was a masterful facilitator of reform, standing on the foundations of his Christian theology. Dr. King sought to shift the social history of America (and the world) by putting his Christian faith into social action.

He brought the concept of "agape love" (to risk loving one's neighbor as you would love yourself, or loving the other without condition) to the forefront of the civil rights movement. According to Dr. King, (An experiment in Love, 1958), "Agape love is not weak, passive love. It is love in action. Agape is seeking to preserve and create community…Agape means a recognition that all life is interrelated. All humanity is involved in a single process and all men are brothers."

King suggested the Beloved Community exists in the here and now; and in the future. The *now* present state of existence (consciously present) and *future* present (not yet consciously recognizable) are mutually connected. This suggests that the present Beloved Community is the building block for the future. And, in order to be created, we must have the sense of its potential presence and act accordingly.

Dr. King was very clear that the means (the protests, marches, sit-ins, and even the boycotts) were simply strategies enacted to bring us to the end, which is the creation of the beloved community - the movement from protest to reconciliation.

According to author Charles Marsh, *The Beloved Community: How Faith Shapes Social Justice, From the Civil Rights Movement to Today,* "The pursuit of the Beloved Community gave the civil rights movement its sustaining spiritual vision...making the teachings of Jesus come alive in the segregated south." Christian theology was the source for this "Christ-shaped love" that could bring about the "Kingdom of God" on earth – the Beloved Community.

I was a young child when the world (not just America) was ALIVE with causes and struggles for justice and equality. My elders and peers were wrapped up in a mighty cause to put an end to oppression and segregation - struggling to rid America once and for all of the laws upholding the practice of *"separate but equal"*. Inspired by the sit-ins, marches, and amazing acts of courage to withstand white oppression by *"Negroes"* from coast to coast: women were burning their bras and demanding equality; the American Indian Movement was birthed, and put new energy into standing up and demanding self-determination among Native Americans and international recognition of their treaty rights; Kwame Nkrumah was leading African countries into independence as Ghana's first elected Prime Minister - over thirty other African countries would soon follow; Nelson Mandela was imprisoned; the Caribbean, Asia, and India were all standing up to colonial governments and demanding their independence; poetry and music rang out with *We Shall Over Come, Give Peace A Chance, What's Going On, Say it Loud—I'm Black and I'm Proud, Inner City Blues...* amid shouts of *I Have A Dream, Black Power, Red Power, Participatory Democracy, Women's Power, Chicano Power* ... This period (1960's - 1970's) felt spontaneous, emotional, passionate, ALIVE! Change was in the air.

Where is the Beloved Community today? It is as though we won the battles but lost the war. Following the death of Dr. Martin Luther King, Jr. and other leaders of the movement, the death toll (Malcom X, Medgar Evers, Jimmie Lee Jackson, Fred Hampton, to name a few), coupled with criminalization of civil rights leaders, resulting in imprisonment and character assassinations of current and would be leaders, proved to be too much. The divide and conquer strategy of government and subversive underground groups affected successfully caused fatigue, disillusionment, and fragmentation of the civil rights era.

We (Black, White, Red, Christian, Jews, Muslims, Indigenous, Women and Men, rich and poor, north and south, organized labor, etc.) shifted from the vision of the Beloved Community, visible by the physical imagery (life in black and white and then color on television sets in people's home for the first time), holding hands and interlocking arms (so much a part of the marches, sit-ins and victory celebrations of the movement), to retreating back into our corners, where we could better articulate our own issues, with our own voices, and affect our own victories. While we raised our voices and our fists for our separate causes, we forgot to create ways and means for us to continue the struggle together, as the Beloved Community - to move from struggle to victory. We became trapped in an old consciousness of separation, in our individual needs, and stopped taking risks to be inclusive. This began the unraveling of the idea of the Beloved Community at its most potent time.

In the midst of writing *Awakening the Heart of the Beloved Community*, my hearts skips a few beats as I realize the "dark night of the soul" of our current "place" in the passion for conscious evolution. I linger sometimes with the feeling that so many got left behind as we became so politically correct that we forgot how to tell the truth, so 'new age' that we refused to see the escalating numbers of young men and women being shackled and placed in prisons - out of sight and out of mind; so cautious we stopped venturing beyond the safety nets of our safe spaces.

Our confusion created fiction parading as truth, but now the calls, the eyes, the vast populations of the poor, those entrapped in mass incarceration, migrant workers, women and children being sold in sex trafficking, truth of those who are the victims of our break away from the Beloved Community, is blaring in our ears and in plain sight. In our minds we are stumped as to how to respond; but, on those days when we listen, really listen to our hearts, we start to feel, and we start to reach out to one another. We come together to march, to walk, to embrace because now we know the only way to save us all, and Mother Earth, is joining together, heart to heart, lifting our voices, and standing together for change on every level. We are *awakening!* We are looking for our Beloved Community because we are ready; and, change is knocking on our doors.

Yesterday, I was at the Selma 50th Anniversary Bridge Crossing in honor of those foot soldiers who put their lives on the line for freedom fifty years ago, on a day that became known as "Bloody Sunday." As I stood at the top of the bridge and looked in all directions and saw unbroken lines of people - thousands, walking together for change - I saw the "awakening" going on. It is here. It is now. And, if we are willing to remain centered in the deeper truth of faith – all faiths and all spiritual traditions - we will realize we are in the midst of the promises of transformation, the awakening of the Heart of the Beloved Community.

As we come together this time, we must create a loving space for ALL of us to enter the circle. Attempting to define the Beloved Community is as elusive as trying to define love - even Agape love. I am not speaking intellectually. I am speaking of the sense of the Beloved Community that captures us and pulls us in to create something better, because we are better.

No matter how articulate I try to be here, when I attempt to define the deep meaning of the Beloved Community that pulled me in, something gets lost in translating its meaning on the pages here. But, oh, does it call to me.

In many ways, the attempt is like trying to catch a butterfly. The moment you capture it to admire its beauty, you realize your error – its beauty is its flight. That is how I feel about the Beloved Community – the moment I attempt to say what it is, I do not do justice to the fact that its potency is far beyond the "it." It is everything that is of "it" – people, nature, cultures, creativity, its peace, and its struggle for what is right/what is just. Its very essence is its flight, as it expands itself to draw all of it in.

In this book about the Beloved Community, the voices of the circle speak; and, we have the opportunity to listen with ears and hearts wide open, for we are the Beloved Community awakening and finding our way to each other.

Part One
THE AWAKENING

1

WE ARE NOW CO-CREATING THE FUTURE

By Kahontakwas Diane Longboat, M.Ed.

We are no longer a minority of disparate voices separated by distance, languages, faiths, or cultures. Our future is not determined by social deficits, but by our resilience and collective strength, our belief in power of the Creator.

We have become the majority, seeking unconditional love, building a peaceful society, shifting to an equitable economy where all thrive believing in abundance, designing a socially just community of caring peoples, making a safe community for men, women, and children, giving space to respectful and dignified living surroundings for Elders, committing to healthful lifestyles, balanced mental health, and faith traditions that uphold the Original Instructions for Life and respect for Creation.

This is the NEW WORLD. It is prayed for, and it is already in place in the future. We, as individuals, must fulfill our individual missions and work each day, collectively, with our respective gifts, to co-create the reality that is waiting for us. We, the living, may not see it in its fullness. Our grandchildren certainly will.

The new world is well on its way. We, as an human family, have reached the tipping point of creating positive change.

Each of us has a mission. Part of that mission is self-discovery. We need to understand why we are living in this time and place, what are our gifts that we can share with the world, what gives meaning to our lives, what are the challenges facing us, and how do we defeat negativity so that it does not cripple us from completing the great spiritual mission that each of us hold?

The relationship that we seek is not only with each other in families, clans, or Nations. Part of the significant relationship that will shape our destiny is feeling the brotherhood/sisterhood with all of humanity, the richness of differences among us, how we can learn so much from each other. We need to celebrate diversity in all of its magic and excitement, revealing other dimensions of knowledge as learn from each other, and celebrate how beautiful the Creator made the human family.

The meaning of relationship that we seek is twofold. The most significant part of relationship falls within the realm of the Sacred. We must be guided spiritually by the Creator through daily conversations that reveal the way forward with joy, love, and fearlessness. The love of the Creator for His Creation and the love of Creation for the Creator is ONE AND THE SAME.

The second part of the relationship means falling in love with Creation. The Code of Life is written on the land. The secrets of relationship, balance, kinship, the meaning of life, and the primary values of love and respect are visible in our sacred homelands.

What is your relationship to the wind, the mineral life, the animal life, plant life, the waters, and the Thunderers who bring rain? Those who fall in love with creation will always stand to defend it. There is only one Mother Earth. The prime directive is to protect and ensure the continuance of Life on this planet.

A GREAT ALIGNMENT IS OCCURRING NOW. Human Beings are aligning with the Beings of the Natural World and the Beings of the Spirit World. We are no longer a minority but a great majority. When our mission is in alignment with that of the Creator for the continuance of Life, we will be successful in creating a NEW WORLD no matter what the odds may be that stand against us.

We are now co-creating the future.

Kahontakwas Diane Longboat, Turtle Clan, Mohawk Nation, Six Nations of the Grand River, Ohsweken, Ontario Canada, M.Ed., brings a wealth of wisdom and experience with over 40 years of work on First Nations education initiatives that includes serving as the National Director of Research for the Assembly of First Nations, the Director of the

Office of Aboriginal Student Services and Programs at the University of Toronto, and consultant to First Nations in numerous areas, including jurisdictional issues in education. She has been involved in assisting communities/ organizations with forming Elders Councils, mediation, rites of passage, and traditional healing practices. Presently, Diane is the ceremonial leader of Soul of the Mother Healing Lodge at Six Nations, Elder and Traditional Healer for the Centre for Addiction and Mental Health (CAMH), and teaches at several academic institutions including the Carl Jung Institute in Zurich, Switzerland. Diane has also published articles/documents for the Royal Commission on Aboriginal Peoples, Journal of Native Studies and the Assembly of First Nations.

2

LOVE: THE ULTIMATE PEACEMAKER

By Michael Bernard Beckwith

How fitting it is to compose this article on a day when millions of individuals are participating in festivities honoring the life and contributions of Dr. Martin Luther King, Jr. Membership in what he coined as the "Beloved Community" continues to find a home in countless lives, acknowledging our interconnectedness as a global family.

Stopping the cycle of violence begins in our relationship with ourselves, which informs how we relate to others, our community, and the larger world. If we have a nuclear war going on within our own mind, we may expect to have a corresponding battleground in our interactions with others, with life itself. It was another harbinger of peace, Mohandas K. Gandhi, who said, "If one does not practice nonviolence in one's personal relations with others and hopes to use it in bigger affairs, one is vastly mistaken." Now is the moment for each of us to open our minds and hearts in great honesty with ourselves. Perhaps we are convinced that our personal abhorrence of violence prevents us from practicing it. Upon closer observation, however, we can catch ourselves practicing subtle forms of violence such as gossiping, sending mental bombs of judgment, anger, resentment, or prejudice towards a particular person, gender, sexual orientation, religion, race, or culture. When such violence expresses, it pollutes the atmosphere with toxins of hatred, aggression, and harm.

One of the major benefits of social media is its achievement in turning the planet into a global village, allowing persons from one nation to protest human injustices and wars taking place in another, as well as supporting individuals who are taking a courageous stand for human rights, oftentimes risking their lives. A perfect example is Malala Yousafzai, who publicly fought for her right and that of other girls to an education. On October 9, 2012, while heading home in a school van she was shot in the head by the Taliban, sparking an international outpouring of support and prayers. And in an unprecedented gesture, the Pakistani army and the government came together to save her life. Her book, *I Am Malala*, became a *New York Times* bestseller, and in 2013, at the age of 16, she became the youngest person ever nominated for a Nobel Peace Prize.

Agents of change including Mahatma Gandhi, Dr. Martin Luther King Jr., Mother Teresa, Nelson Mandela, Rev. James M. Lawson, Jr., Cesar Chavez, His Holiness the Dalai Lama, and Dr. A. T. Ariyaratne, to name a few, demonstrate to the world that when the heart is fully open it becomes an instrument of love, of nonviolence. We speak of individuals who change the times and conditions in which they live as being great lovers of humankind. Their lives are living proof that justice, equality, and peace are ignited by love. To have more love we must understand, as they did, that our true nature is love. To discern that our true nature is love is to know that we are created in the very image and likeness of Love, the essence of Life itself.

Through our individual inner work and spiritual practices, we discover that we have innate gifts to contribute to the creation of an enlightened society. We then become motivated to deliver these gifts in a mindset and heart-set of love, rather that out of fear that the world needs saving. We are not here to "save" the world; we are here to serve an emerging paradigm of love, compassion, and generosity of heart.

The Beloved Community is based on the awareness that we are One, not simply when we hold hands and sing the song "We Are the World," but when we live by the universal spiritual principle of Oneness. The inner work we are called to do is as significant as all those who have set the example of what it means to be an emissary of love, peace, compassion, justice, and loving-kindness. Let us, too, set our aspiration to become an active architect in service to the Beloved Community.

Each of us is a choice-point in the center of the universe. What will be your choice? Are you willing to cultivate a heart of love as wide as the world? As world citizens, we have the opportunity to proclaim that now is the time to bring a halt to dehumanizing our global brothers and sisters, that now is the time to put an end to wars, world hunger, inadequate health care, lack of education, and violating Mother Nature. The world is looking for love masters. *Each and every one of us is that potential lover master.*

Michael Bernard Beckwith is the founder of Agape International Spiritual Center, a community of thousands of local members and worldwide live streamers. In 2012, he addressed the UN General Assembly during its annual World Interfaith Harmony Conference. Beckwith co-chairs the Gandhi King Season for Nonviolence, which was launched at the United Nations in 1998. He has appeared on *Dr. Oz, The Oprah Winfrey Show, OWN Help Desk, Tavis Smiley,* and *Larry King Live.*

Part Two

THE ARTS

3

THE ARTS AND OUR BELOVED COMMUNITY

By Karen Hunter Watson

As an artist, I have always believed that music and art are major components to building community. They are very important for our daily growth. It is well known that people of all walks of life, from different cultures, all include art and/or music in their lives. There is something happening within humankind that is bringing about a change in our universe. And in that change, the arts play an important role.

When you hear a beautiful song, it touches something inside of you; just as when you look at a piece of art, it can bring emotional feelings to you. Music has been used as a successful key to communication. An example of that was the time I was in Mexico with the Trail of Dreams World Peace Walk.

One morning, while we were in a park in Mexico, we saw a man who was whistling and swinging his lunch bucket walking down the street. We had spent the night in the park, and were entering the day full of excitement about being in Mexico. When he approached us I said, "Buenos Dias Senior," which was the extent of my Spanish. He responded in Spanish, and began to carry on a conversation; and, I said, "Poquito Espanol," and he laughed good-naturedly. I had told him I spoke very little Spanish.

I began to communicate with him in a way that proved to be very successful, as neither one of us could speak the others language, and that was by using sign language. It is the method that got us around the world. We learned that he was a radio announcer on his way home; and, when he found out that we were walking around the world for peace he got very excited, and wanted to talk about us on his radio show.

I'm not quite sure how it got started; but, before I knew it, he was singing and I was singing and we had a wonderful time. He later invited us to have lunch with him,, and we learned that he was a monk that was taking a hiatus from the monastery because of the death of his son; and, he needed time to heal. He was a delightful person; and, we enjoyed each other's company through good food and wonderful music most of the afternoon.

Music was the key. It helped to open up all of our hearts in order for us to better communicate. That is the gift of music; it has a language of its own, and it is expressed and carried to the hearts of those who will hear it. To me, that was the perfect example of beloved community. This man knew nothing about us, yet he invited five people into his home to share a meal with him; and, when we got there, he serenaded us while we ate. Amazing!

My journey around the world for peace has taught me that people are the same all over the planet. We want to provide for our families, live our lives in peace, keep our families safe, have access to good food, and live in harmony with one another and our planet. Our communication helps us to see our similarities instead of our differences. It helps us to see that we are a community; we are alike.

In our travels, we created to merge with communities around the world. These were communities that did not look at the color of our skin, but only the content of our character. Nor did it matter that we could not speak the same language, only that we displayed peace and love in our communication with them. This is my idea of beloved community. A community based on love and respect for all from all.

When we first went into Mexico, we were warned not to trust anyone, not to drive at night because something may happen to us. Thank God we did not take their warning because what we found was that people responded to how they were treated which was with kindness and respect. And their willingness to help us was just what we needed, because we were constantly in need of their assistance, not knowing the country. This was another example of beloved community.

It took the help of people all around the world to get us from one place to the other, because our walk was totally a faith walk. When we started, we had just enough money to last us for two weeks, but we had just enough faith to last us a lifetime; and, with the help of people who cared, we traveled all around the world. We found our beloved community. We found people who loved us enough to help us, provide for us, take us into their homes, eat their food, be with their children, and genuinely accepted us for who we are.

And, because of that, we see them as our extended family. I have children all around the world, brothers and sisters, aunts and uncles, grandmothers and grandfathers; people who love me just because of who I am, beloved community. People of different cultures, different colors, who speak different languages, have different names, different religions, yet one community…the community of love.

If I were to define Beloved Community, I would say it means: people coming together as they are, being accepted for their differences as they are, and giving and receiving love, knowing it is alright to be different. I have experienced this over and over again in life. The arts have been helpful tools to begin this healing process that is opening and cleansing the hearts of people all over the planet who are different yet alike. We are the Beloved Community.

Karen Hunter Watson is a native of Illinois who now resides in Alabama. She is a songwriter, vocalist, visual artist, author, a non-denominational ordained minister, a peace activist, and a peace walker who walked around the world for peace.

4

MY BELOVED COMMUNITY
By Joy Jinks

My *beloved community* is the little town where I was born, and still live, Colquitt, Georgia. Since Dr. King coined the phrase "The Beloved Community," it has become embedded in my consciousness. Several years ago, I had a colorful sign painted with these words, and placed in the corner of my front yard, proclaiming my passion and mission for every passer-by to see.

The Church quotes Jesus Christ as saying that the Kingdom of Heaven is among us; and, the message of Dr. King is the same. The beloved community is here when we recognize it, and see the importance of each citizen. It is the longed for Promised Land that we seek to create, the land of peace and plenty, abundance and harmony. Colquitt, Georgia is the place where I have purposed to build the infrastructure of the beloved community to be a living demonstration, and to be a working model.

In my community, I was witnessing an ever-widening gap between what was needed, both materially and spiritually, by people, and what was available to them. And, I became aware of a poverty of spirit that can manifest in racism, violence, sexism, crime, and addiction. The goal of our beloved community is to empower citizens to claim their rightful place by honoring each other, celebrating people's unique gifts, and creating a sense of pride of place.

Over the years, many community projects were initiated which attempted to fulfill these goals, to offer job training in the form of a school for Licensed Practical Nurses, after-school pro-grams, as well as early education and daycare for children of the working poor. A manufacturing plant for mayhaw jelly was begun as a means of providing employment, and to popularize an indigenous fruit. Still, we do not live by bread alone, but by beauty in its many forms. The beautiful Tarrer Inn, a bed and breakfast inn, was the first symbol of the revitalization of Colquitt. Beautiful surroundings enrich people's spirit, and speak of their value as human beings.

Colquitt honors the lives of its people by recording their stories and presenting them in a biannual production called Swamp Gravy. For 22 years, the stage in Cotton Hall has been filled with local volunteer actors singing and telling the stories of their community. Colquitt has become a national model for community development through Art and Culture. But more importantly, the lives of ordinary people are validated as we share the agony and the ecstasy of the human experience.

The beautiful murals, which hide the ugly, crumbling walls of downtown buildings, set the tone of our town, and send subliminal messages while depicting our values of neighborliness, fun, cooperation, peace, and beauty. Our love of nature is fed by our Spring Creek Park, which is like an outdoor cathedral where the natural world blesses us with its beauty. The flowing water beckons us to be at peace.

The casual visitor is intrigued by these outward and visible signs that there is something different about this little town. But the new spirit is best manifest as the boundaries that separate people are crossed, such as welcoming inmates from the local jail to worship with their families on Sunday morning in the local Methodist church, and to join the voluntary 12-step program on Sunday nights. In such a setting, pain is shared and joys are celebrated by the wider community.

As we live in communities, large or small, urban or rural, may we endeavor to create heaven on earth, and communities where everyone is beloved.

Joy Sloan Jinks is a graduate of Florida State University with a Master's in Social Work. As a community organizer, she has been involved community and economic development in her hometown for over 30 years. Her most notable achievement has been as founder of Swamp Gravy, Georgia's Folk Life Play that has become a national model for economic development through the Arts and Culture. In 2015, Swamp Gravy is celebrating its 23rd year of performances, and its role in the development of cultural tourism as an industry. She is organizer of the Tenth Annual Building Creative Communities conference that brings "Cultural Creatives" together to share best practices in using the

Arts as an avenue for social change. www.bccconference-colquittga.com. She has had a diverse career as a social worker in public welfare and in mental health services, as well as an entrepreneur in organizing a woman-owned gourmet food manufacturing company, The Mayhaw Tree.

She has received the Governor's Award in the Humanities, the Georgia Trend magazine's "100 Most Influential Georgians," and a Lifetime Achievement Award from the Colquitt/Miller Chamber of Commerce. In addition to speaking about the Power of the Arts and Story in community development, she is writing a book called Dynamic Aging, to be published in the Fall 2015.

5

STORYTELLING: HOW IT HELPS BUILD THE BELOVED COMMUNITY

By Janet WindWalker Jones

In 1957, Dr. Martin Luther King said "the aftermath of nonviolence is the creation of the beloved community, while the aftermath of violence is tragic bitterness." He spoke of the importance of building a worldwide beloved community, defined as a place where international standards of human decency will no longer allow poverty, hunger, and homelessness to be tolerated. In that beloved community, racism and all other forms of social injustice that flourish in a world based on fear, born of violence and bitterness, will be replaced by an all-inclusive spirit of sister and brotherhood – a worldwide family of loving beings working together for the ongoing benefit of humankind.

The book, *Letters to Friends: Wisdom Through Storytelling*, published early in 2015, puts forth the hypothesis that storytelling is the foundation of all communication since the beginning of time, and builds trust and understanding among all beings, thus helping dismantle fear, distrust, intolerance, and injustice. It invites people everywhere to return to sharing their stories as a powerful teaching tool just as our indigenous ancestors did.

When people share their stories, they find themselves moving toward, discovering, and/or maintaining a spiritual centering in their lives that supports the development of the beloved community of Dr. King's vision. Sharing personal stories opens the heart of the storyteller in a way that the listener can hear with their heart also; thus opening the heart of the listener to share as well, and together they engage in conversation that goes beyond words, into the very spirit of both their beings. In this manner we learn from, inspire and support one another as fellow members of the family of humankind.

I remember when I was small, hearing stories I heard as personal rejection, because my mother said, "That's not my baby, I'm a white lady," when I was brought to her at birth. Later, because I was so much darker than either my sister or brother, and I was brown eyed while they were blue eyed, my brother repeated words he didn't even understand, naming me "niggaheene". It stung! He was young, and meant no harm, but I hurt deeply. From that experience, I was able to connect to how others who were discriminated against on the basis of color felt. Early in life, this knowledge helped me walk a social justice path for all. We're all part of the same human family, and an analysis of the stories in the above noted book shows that the themes running through our life stories have much in common, regardless of the personal cultural differences among us. As a result, we are all, therefore, able to learn from one another, and grow in connectedness as we do.

Many people, me included, have spoken to, taught about, and written of the great value of storytelling in our lives, and how it was passed down in our families, generation after generation, as a powerful learning tool, capable of imparting great wisdom, understanding and support. As I have traveled around the Americas and to other continents, I have witnessed it being used by indigenous cultures, the world over, to pass on wisdom and teach about virtues like kindness, trust, sharing, and love. Storytelling allows barriers between people, built from fear, to dissolve, and be replaced by a web of caring and connectedness. This web weaves across generations and cultures, and stretches across the boundaries of time and worlds, bringing us together as one people. It is in such loving ways we can, as collective members of the family of humankind, work together to dispel fear and distrust across cultures and continents, erase violence, and bring about global peace, forming a worldwide beloved community of people who love and respect ourselves and others, and who live one in relationship with mother earth, and people everywhere. One might think of storytelling as a "key" that unlocks a door.
Storytelling creates images of a person's experience that allows the listener to see, hear, and "feel" it; it allows the listener to relate to others by connecting the stories shared to their own world of experience. In this

way, one person's "lessons learned" provides affirmation for others, and/or becomes the roadmap for discovery in another person's life. As this phenomenon occurs, fear diminishes and understanding takes its place. Those who once feared "difference" begin to see embracing it and learning from it as a way to expand their own possibilities, and it becomes highly valued instead. Just as violence begets violence, loving, caring actions beget harmony; and, harmony begets harmony. In this ongoing fashion, storytelling helps build the foundation for a worldwide family of loving beings working together for the ongoing benefit of humankind. It is a vital practice for all of us to engage in. The programs and people working to build a beloved community benefit in their work by the use of storytelling. It is a wonderful, healing medicine that stretches across generations and worlds, healing across time, and helping to lay a new foundation for benevolent communities well into the future.

Janet WindWalker Jones is Long Hair Clan Mother to the Cherokee in Texas, and a member of the Texas Cherokee Tribe. She has ancestral ties to the the Lenne Lenape and Wabanaki People, the Creek Nation, the Scott-Irish, Newfoundlanders, and English. She celebrates and honors multiculturalism as one of the fundamental tenants of community. She is lead author on a recent book in publication on Storytelling called "Letters to Friends: Wisdom Through Storytelling."

6

STORY BRIDGE
By Richard Owen Geer and Jules Corriere

In the 1960s, theater for social change consisted of performances against injustice. Playwrights, directors, and actors staged the stories of oppressed others. And, most of the time, that's as far as it went. A decade later, when Richard first noticed the power of performance to build community among his casts, he didn't realize he was in the vanguard of a new kind of socially active theater.

This new form moved performance toward participation - people are affected more by what they experience, than by what they observe. When he directed a play, he noticed two important outcomes: first, the play, and second, the community the players become. This very special sort of theater community is called "ensemble." Generous, creative, playful, and spontaneous, an ensemble of actors love each other, their audience, the theater, and the act of creating together. A question arose that would eventually direct both the lives of Richard Geer and Jules Corriere:

"What if a rehearsal room was as big as a community? What sort of a community could that become?"

NOT IN MY BACKYARD

In Uptown Chicago, Bill owned a gorgeous, upscale condo in a mixed-income neighborhood. It was the early 90's, and the beginning of the generation of the area. During this time, Uptown was notorious for being the last stop on the line for those leaving jails and mental hospitals; so, there were many people on the streets, and many single room occupancy buildings (SROs) to house the formerly homeless. Groups formed to push this element out of the neighborhood, often called "NIMBY" (Not In My Back Yard) organizations. Bill headed one of these. He wanted to protect the investment he worked hard for, he wanted to transform the "social service ghetto" that he and others saw Uptown becoming.

The Community Performance project Scrap Mettle SOUL (SMS) formed during this period. SMS's mission was to present stories of urban life (SOUL) from the entire community, including the homeless. There was so much diversity: the homeless, those supporting the homeless, those opposed, those who supported the police, those who were out to expose police corruption, little ethnic enclaves speaking over one hundred languages, and families of every kind trying to make a living and raise their kids. A gateway community, Uptown, 040, has been called the most diverse zip code in the United States. In the middle of this stood Scrap Mettle SOUL, literally in the middle, because SMS did not take sides. In it, you would find Bill, passionately telling the story of his days building

IBM as an executive, and building a life for himself and his wife in this neighborhood he loved so much; you would also meet Geraldine, a former bag lady, who found Uptown to be the neighborhood where she felt most comfortable. You'd also meet Barbara, an amazing organizer, who's economic situation led her to live in subsidized housing; Stephan, a brilliant PhD, bi-polar, formerly homeless; and Joe who lived in the SRO that Bill was trying to close.

Bill and Joe were cast to sing a duet. Center stage, the NIMBY Bill singing with the SRO chap he didn't want in his backyard; in turn, politically active Joe, dancing with "the man."

As the two rehearsed, a relationship formed. Instead of saying "you're wrong" for thinking this way, each one, in the context of safety and trust that the work provided, was able to appreciate the other. Stories emerged. Questions arouse, along with a sincere desire to learn about the other. "Bill, why don't you want me in your neighborhood?" With the first question, people, not postures, started to speak.

Bill did not leave his NIMBY organization. And Joe did not stop his political action. But, things changed at a personal level. Joe was able to see Bill other than as the enemy. They would even meet and have lunch. Bill saw Joe, Stephan, and Barbara, not as subsidized housing residents, but as people. He recognized Barbara's skills and referred her to a better paying job, and this allowed her to keep the home she was about to lose.

The individual connections allowed change to happen - person to person. It was not a revolution; but, it was life changing for those individuals, as they moved from "I" to "We."

A STORY WORTH LIVING

Story, shared in community, offers believable, meaningful, emotional proof of a deep truth: when things integrate, their optimal functionality is revealed. Story integrates people, events, and places into a meaningful whole. Fully to integrate the heart into the body is to connect it to every artery, vein, and capillary, enabling it, perfectly, to perform. The story-to-change process, from strangers to change-makers, encourages this quality of relationship. When each person in the group feels safe, free, and charged with enthusiasm to share, in fullness, her full self while the others deeply listen, and ditto for everyone else, then we are in a perfect circulatory system, and every heartbeat affects everything everywhere.

From Alienation to Community Action
Copyright 2012, Community Performance, Inc.
Richard Owen Geer and Jules Corriere
Illustrated by Nancy Sylvia
with Melissa Block, Juanita Brown, David Isaacs and the
Learning Community of the Jonesborough Yarn Exchange

Dr. Richard Geer created Community Performance – Theater of, by, and for the community – to empower individuals and bring neighborhoods together. Geer has founded over a score of Community Performance groups, including Georgia's Official Folk Life play, "Swamp Gravy", part of the Cultural Olympiad in Atlanta, Georgia, and also featured at the Kennedy Center in Washington, DC. In partnership with the International Storytelling Center, Geer and CPI are pioneering ways to bring this transformational work to organizations and communities nationwide. His work has been showcased across America, as well as in England, Scotland, Brazil, and Chile. Geer holds a PhD. in Performance Studies from Northwestern University.

Jules Corriere has written thirty-eight plays, edited a book of oral histories, and recently completed a season writing and directing a monthly radio-variety show. Her production of Scrap Mettle SOUL's "The Whole World Gets Well" won the Presidential Points of Light Award and toured in London and Edinburgh. Other playwright credits include "Let My People Go! A Spiritual Journey" which performed at the Kennedy Center Concert Hall; and "Turn the Wash Pot Down" in Union, SC, featured in People Magazine and named by the state legislature as the First Official Folk Life Play of the state. She appears in the 2010-2011 edition of Who's Who for her work in the field on Theater Arts and Social Activism.

7

THE INHERITANCE OF THE HIP HOP GENERATION

By Mikuak Rai

"Our goal is to create a beloved community and this will require a qualitative change in our souls as well as a quantitative change in our lives."

Every time Dr. Martin Luther King, Jr. evoked his vision of a beloved community, he sent a small ripple of consciousness forth into the ether to be carried to future generations on vibrations of light, yet to become manifest in the fullness of form. A visionary as well as a catalyst, the ripples of his self-awareness and responsibility to humanity have, over the past nearly 50 years since his sudden death, grown to a crescendo and cresting wave powered by the force of Love, the very Love that King served so humbly and fervently. Who would have predicted at the close of the 60's that the next generation to inherit King's calling would do so at a pulpit comprised of two turntables and a microphone, with congregants no longer convened in church buildings, but instead, at block parties?

With the advent of Hip Hop Culture, born in the South Bronx in the 1970s, the baton of the beloved community vision was passed along to a new generation of young voices, minds, and bodies in search of outlets to express their youthful creativity and wise-beyond-their-years social discontent. Much like the Civil Rights Movement before them, Hip Hop Culture was essentially rooted in non-violence; effectiveness of rappers and DJs was measured by who could move the crowd and keep the party 'live.' Street gangs throughout NYC marked their turf with graffiti and faced off against each other through rap-battles and b-boy dance competitions, opting for creativity as opposed to self-destructive violent eruption.

By the early 80s, Hip Hop musical elements found their way into popular songs played on radio, such as "Rapture" by Blondie, which topped the U.S. Billboard Hot 100. In 1982, Melle Mel and Duke Bootee wrote "The Message", which initiated the inclusion of 'conscious' lyrics in Hip Hop, paving the way for a torrent of socially aware and culturally centered recording artists for years to come. Several Hip Hop-themed films emerged between 1982-85, expanding the realm of the culture far beyond New York City. By 1984, a global phenomenon was underway, propelled by youth audiences worldwide. Hip Hop would soon be universal.

The evolving spirit and force of Love will always be challenged by elements of fear and resistance to change. Throughout the American South during the 1950s and 60s, when Black people protested and boycotted to bring an end to the era of so-called Jim Crow laws, they were met with heinous attacks carried out by those unwilling to change. Similarly, a generation later, the consciousness movement in Hip Hop, known as the 'Golden Age', that served to educate and mobilize Black urban youth in America to stand up to police brutality, social inequality, and the perpetuation of drugs and violence throughout their communities, would come under attack. However, this time the perpetuators were not as easily identifiable; yet, the effect of the intentional silencing of the love-motivated, culturally conscious artist and orator became very evident.

A new facade was erected to replace the previously burgeoning movement of empowerment and social awareness. This abhorrent turn, that used Hip Hop Culture as its vehicle, witnessed the degradation and dismantling of many generations worth of work and advancement. The glorification of a materialistic mindset and a 'thug' mentality, set against a backdrop of Black-on-Black violence and pervasive hatred against women, would set the tone for the majority of the 1990's and our entry well into the new millennium. Naive consumers and experts/commentators alike would reference the now-usurped art form to validate both mockery and scorn of an entire culture and population. Of course, a celebrated few would rise to 'the top' and enormously benefit from the exploitation of their own people, shunning any real sense of responsibility and artistic integrity, all in the name of 'art imitates life.' By now, the beloved community would seem to be far beyond reach and recognition, with Dr. King's foresight and instruction falling on deaf ears, drowned out by an information age overstocked with disposable instantaneity, and wanting for wisdom.

Then, thankfully, something happened. Like Q-Tip, from the legendary Hip Hop group, A Tribe Called Quest, states in his opening verse on the song *Excursions*, "I said, well, Daddy, don't you know that things go in cycles?" After being diminished and nearly forgotten by a generation, the vision and essence of the beloved community has experienced a great resurgence in the recent past, due to a variety of factors.

One such factor is that the recording industry machine, which once reigned supreme, and was able to manufacture 'reality' and project popular opinion to its own benefit (even if it meant the exploitation of an authentic art form, the over-saturation of dull and ordinary life on earth rather than spiritual things and the perpetuation of negative stereotypes), has been replaced by more decentralized methods of music production, broadcast, and distribution. This shift has enabled and given voice to many more people than ever before, who are using positive Hip Hop as a medium of expression and vehicle for social justice, cross-cultural understanding, reconciliation, and a renewal of the human spirit, worldwide.

Another factor we have witnessed is that, due to the information age and the Internet, the millennial generation is far more informed, aware, and advanced than previous generations insofar as having an astute perspective on the inequities and injustices that exist among the global community. A case in point is the Arab Spring revolution of late 2010 that swept through the Middle East, and subsequently gave rise to the Occupy Wall Street Movement and International Occupy Movement which saw millions of people engaged in peaceful protest against social and economic inequality. The nonviolent response of millions of people to both the Ferguson, Missouri shooting death of unarmed teenager Michael Brown and the choking death of Eric Garner in Staten Island, New York, both of them Black men, and both killed at the hands of police officers, has completely reinvigorated a movement that reaches from the grassroots of rural and urban communities to the President's administration and beyond, echoing the declaration that #BlackLivesMatter.

And more recently, the Golden Globe and Oscar-nominated film "Selma", directed by African American filmmaker Ava DuVernay, brings back into focus the legacy and shoulders upon which our contemporary human rights movements stand. Nearly all of the demonstrations mentioned above exhibited something important to note… references to Dr. King and the Civil Rights Movement, and the presence of Hip Hop music in some form, fashion, and expression.

I assert that the realization of the beloved community is the inheritance and responsibility of the Hip Hop generation; this now-generation of young parents, families, youth, grandparents, artists, educators, stewards, visionaries, entrepreneurs, creatives, and leaders. With every tool and technology at our disposal, and with the appropriate effort, guidance, intelligence, persistence, and fortitude, there is no reason why, other than for a lack of will, Dr. King's mountaintop revelation of April 3rd, 1968 cannot be made real in this time and space. The prophesied Promised Land is at hand; no longer just a dream, the beloved community is coming more and more into tangible and visceral form. This qualitative change in our souls and the quantitative change in our lives that King speaks of is what beckons to us now. After all, we are the ones we've been waiting for. And, ultimately, it will be "unarmed truth and unconditional love that will have the final word in reality."

In Hip Hop there's an ongoing discussion about which Emcee/rapper is the G.O.A.T. (Greatest of All Time). If we're being honest with ourselves, we may just want to humbly defer to Dr. King, the orator and Master of Ceremonies who toasted the global party best, just one decade before the birth of what we now call Hip Hop. With his immediately recognizable tone and articulate pentameter, an archive of quotes that has no end, a vision that called to the future, and a legacy that will live on forever, it could be argued that there is none better. And, if ever you require some inspiration and motivation, go online and listen to King's speech, "I've Been to the Mountaintop." Like the crowd, you will be moved.

Mikuak Rai is a self-described creative catalyst. He is the founder and creative director of WorldBridge Media, a multimedia and event production consulting and technical services provider. Mikuak uses his skills and talents to support a wide range of social and spiritual movements including the URI Global Indigenous Network, Nexus Global Youth Summit, Planet Restoration, the 13 Moon Calendar Change/Natural Time Peace Movement, Project Blue Hands, Heal Humanity, and the global Dalit Civil Society movement. A visionary singer/songwriter, musician, and composer, Mikuak has been fortunate to record and perform his own original music, tour globally, and collaborate with many talented musical artists, of diverse backgrounds, from around the world. Contact him via email at worldbridgemedia@gmail.com, and follow him on Twitter: @mikuakrai

8

LUCK
By Sejahari Saulter-Villegas

There is a crusade between my people and this casino

We gamble in a plight where it is unordinary to be alive

Designed on our lack of luck

Luck

An in-cohesive collection of questions that comes in the casino

With such a cash coming consequence
It is when the smell of success scratches the nostril of every oxygen
Molecule in the vicinity

But when your odds are as slim as starving revolutions

Luck becomes as quiet as Sunday mornings before funerals
And if you'd seen the absence of smiles or recurring songs of sirens
On my block you would call me unlucky

Grab coin in-sert pull lever
Wait wait wait JACKPOT!

I hear screaming from the slots
Machines where white men bet on black boy jackpots
Welcomed by the smell of supremacy in the cigarette smoke

The sound of dice dancing on the scabs and skulls of black smiles
Crescendos off of every bluff
Beginners luck

After someone has offered me a drink of corruption
I turn to see rows of concentrated costumers cramming desire in
Their fingers

Like prideful crop pickin' participants playing for their right to live

Grab coin in-sert pull lever
Wait wait wait

For cardboard colored kids get lost in this Vegas with no back up

We are their black jacks
Our lives have become as temporary as a #blacklivesmatter hash tag

The casino has been our place of play since the inception of our
Thievery

Back when boats were homicidal slot machines
Where European men landed jackpots on West African coastlines

Poker faced my people until they were valued as 3/5th of what was
Actually in their hands

Human

And still now
They create white clubs to capture our Kings
Suck our crowns in their American hole

Call it a royal flush

Rules say
In order to get a jackpot all of the pictures in the slots have to be of
The same image

And still the faces of incarcerations have been the same for 300
Years

We have never been considered royal face cards to this casino
Yet this inconsiderate edifice of income has been built on our backs

And our tongues and our lunges and our fist and our fight

And still we are stuck unlucky with no jackpot to rejoice over

As I attempt to make a bet
This casino of a country lands jackpots on our innocence

And call us unlucky
Unlucky is a life being confined in a coco skin killing company

We won't win until we make this game ours
How long will we grab coin in-sert pull lever

Use our sorrow as a sad excuse for political publicity
And watch them play us over and over and over

I still stare at the roulette

They yell out from the arcade section
Across from roulette

Down the way from the poker tables
Right above bingo

Made a casino out of melanin
Gambled flesh

Treat our deaths like an Ace of Spades. Profit
Treat our lives like three of diamonds.

Useless

And there's nothing black boys do better than build broken futures.

Sejahari Amaru Villegas, age 16, was born on a snowy Chicago March 4th day to a African American mother and Mexican Father. His journey would soon be nurtured by an artistic environment as his mother was a founder of an Arts and Education organization in Chicago that exposed him to performance poetry, dance, and theater since the womb. He is a 3-time Illinois State Teen Poetry Champion, and recently placed top 10 in the world! At the early age of 4 he began performing with the Kuumba Lynx Performance Ensemble and has been a main cast member in the WE GET FREE Hip Hop Theater 2014/2015 national tour. Though his lines were simple his talent shined brilliantly. Since his first taste of the stage he has beamed with talent and has graced the stages such as Steppenwolf Theater in Chicago, and videos such as "Watch My Feet" by Hip Hop Artist Dude N Dem.

9

UNPLUGGED

By Tannur "SheWrightz" Ali

I got Unplugged
And found myself plugged in
Came unhinged
And bowed down in submission
I am not the seer of my mission
Just a believer in Greater Powers
Believer in a notion
That love will keep on growing
Even if it's planted in concrete
Ideologies
Even if it's never had a guide
To send it sifting
Through reality
Love is my reality
And you are as sparks to my flame
The ignition
Drenched in heaven sent capacities
To help me know my purpose
I'm worth it
Finally
I'm perfect, eternally
And not in egotistical senses
In extraterrestrial admission
That I have seen GOD
Surviving
Thriving inside all of us
Sending synapse between personas

So all of our actions are from the same thoughts
We all got caught in this morning's
Inspiration
It rained, and once
We got that trust in things unseen
Faith is but a common truss between
The walls of all of this
And thus
We must remain
Unplugged, but plugged in to higher missions
Unhinged, but
Bent down in submission
Reflecting heavenly capacities
All over this thing
And what would you call it?
What visions have called you to listen?
Called you to consensus
With the rest of us
Who know the differences between us are merely
Heavens intentions
For our Gods to know their own purpose
We are but the lessons learned vicariously
By a celestial collective of inherent ambitions
To evolve
I believe in things unseen cause I have
Been blinded by a cause
Deafened by hectic rhetoric
Cast down by the lowest of corrosive spirits
And risen again like a phoenix
Found myself in tune with vibrations
Seen glory between silver linings
And remembered I am not alone here
You too, are on this path
And we are innumerable
We're just so in tune, you know

If it seems like we've been guided
It's only because we have
If it seems like I'm too hype
It's only because I am
This is not the ebb
It's the flow
This is but the time to let go
Curvy currents tend to carry current limits off with ocean
Mystics and ultraviolet visions
Of little lights in dark places
You just need a little heart to start ignition
A little spark to start the engine
You've got to travel kind of far
Outside your comfort zone to find where you belong
And when you get here
I'll be waiting
Making available to you the
Space to come unplugged
And find your mission
Come unhinged, and fling progression
Like the opened gates of heaven
This is
Just our beginning

Tannur "SheWrightz" Ali, originally from Philadelphia, PA, began writing poetry at eight years old and performing at the age of 11 at "Panoramic Poetry" in the October Art Gallery. At the age of fourteen, she self-published a chapbook entitled Rhymin' with Reason. As the founder of iLOGIC ™ (Institute for the Love Of Genius In Communities), Tannur lives her life as a public servant, providing events, workshops, classes and spaces where people can "Get UnPlugged and find themselves plugged in".

As a Social Artist, she uses her talents as a poet, un-schooling mother, gardener, cook, and paperwork lady to help light the path of Self Realization. Her focus is especially on those who are dedicated to their own self-improvement. Tannur works with the Albany Housing Authority to provide a community garden space, as well as community enrichment programs to over 215 households in the Albany, GA area.

Winner of the Judith Stark Creative Writing Award, Host of Unplugged Poetry, creator of Pen Stroke National Poetry Festival, SheWrightz believes in the powers of transparency and vulnerability to transcend what Jean Houston calls "the great divide of other." Her poetry provides a glimpse into her conviction.

Part Three
PERSONAL & COMMUNITY HEALTH

10

PSYCHOLOGICAL PREPAREDNESS:
What Do We Teach Our Youth?
By Mary Elizabeth Hargrow, Ph.D.

I have observed our local communities change more rapidly and profoundly within the last five years than in the prior 10 to 15 years. Some of these changes have double-triple impact on our lives and our psyche sending stress levels through the roof even for individuals and groups unaware that they are worried about the future of our youth, communities, and the planet. One might hear some say, "I don't let any of that bother me because there is nothing that I can do about it anyway".

Many of the changes are monumental and present aspects to be celebrated when interwoven into the fabric of our lives and communities with strong elements of compassion, justice, logic, and love. Most often radical changes involve the potential for chaos and/or progress, rarely if ever is change irrelevant. A short list of personally observed recent and continuing change include: (1) the amount and depth of information and knowledge available in the public domain to everyone with access to the Internet, (2) the speed of communication and the flexible transport of goods and services, (3) the coming together and sharing of ancient medical-healing and cultural practices related to the body-mind/emotion-spirit/soul connections, (4) an expansion of non-food included in the food chain, and added poisons in the water, earth and air, (5) increases in terrorizing inventions, threating communication styles and content, and mind sets that raise threats to peace, justice, and prosperity for local and global communities and (6) a vast explosion in the availability of what I call "the intellectual triad" - information, knowledge, and wisdom-plus the availability of high energy especially in the fields of health, nutrition, and emotional wellbeing.

As we continue our journey as a human species, greater and more profound levels of the intellectual triad is being made available to us to remember and apply in our lives at all levels-the individual, family and community-locally, nationally, and globally.

This incredible accessibility appears directly linked to the species' need to find significantly different ways to 'skin the cat' / find alternative solutions to today's challenges. Could the message for all of us including the youth be - use your gifts and find other ways to be together? Over many millenniums we have tried many ways of being together - enslavement, mass incarceration, long term imprisonment, torture, creating systems where a few get vast amounts of the wealth and others who helped in creating the wealth get very little – a system that generates extremes in wealth and poverty.

Where and how can we find answers to accomplish what is needed for this time? There is evidence that there are currently species on this planet that are older than humans. There is also evidence that the human species has lived on the planet continuously for many millenniums. Much of the "intellectual triad" made available along the way to make this long survival possible is preserved in art, architecture, writing, science - including medicine, healing, mathematics, and other areas. Part of the intellectual triad is also preserved and available in cultural practices and messages from individuals endowed with special talents. They have emerged as teachers and guides that expand our basic human awareness exponentially and help to activate an explosion in individual, group, and global change. Many courses, including history help to unlock critical pathways that can be taken to acquire the content within the intellectual triad.

The human species is arriving at a crossroad of heightened awareness where greater and more profound levels of the intellectual triad are needed, and the content is available in abundance to masses of people globally, from the poor to the elite. Material elitism only guarantees easy access to the intellectual triad, whereas, the economically poor may be deprived of this luxury. Upon acquiring either leg - information or knowledge - internal and external action must be applied to attain wisdom. Applying what we know is one of our greatest challenges. Thinking, perceiving, feeling, and taking action are constantly involved in the psychological processing that form the foundation for community creation and transformation.

Some Wisdom Keepers of Ancient intellectual triads during the time of the conquest of the Americas reveal that to protect the content from being destroyed, much of the knowing being brought forward at this time had to be separated and hidden among different groups - to be brought back together at a time of great need. The time of great need is here now.

A number of individuals have been engaged in the remembering and reconnecting process of the intellectual triad for about three decades. Hence, there are now a number of teachers, guides, healers and centers. More active troops are needed along with holistic curricula reaching more people and establishing learning and healing communities based on the integration of ancient and contemporary knowing.

How can each of us work collectively to create love-based communities that address current, incoming, ongoing, and unknown challenges? The Sankofa bird reminds us to remember and embrace that which has sustained us as we go forward "in love" adding the new. The first part helps us to build a foundation. Without a strong foundation resilience is not possible. Newness alone is not sufficient to withstand the many types of challenges involved in living an ethically engaged life and ethics must be present within all work for it to be credible.

Dr. Cornell West in his book, *The Radical King*, illuminates the kind of resilience, vision, and love required for living a life committed to making the world a more compassionate, generous, and loving place. The new is based in knowledge and wisdom that has evolved over time. Hence, historical knowledge is important - taught in a way that brings the steps in discovering information and acquiring knowledge and wisdom to life. Again, application is the key.

Mary Elizabeth Hargrow, PhD is a past president of The Association of Black Psychologists and licensed psychologist in clinical practice in Los Angeles. She is founder and executive director of Lesedi Wholistic Healing Environments, a non-profit organization focusing on planetary healing using ancient wisdom, diverse knowledge, and contemporary science. She specializes in assisting individuals and families uncover and resolve debilitating emotional pain. She has provided educational and psychological services in settings across racial, ethnic, class and cultural boundaries: an Indian reservation, urban public schools, mental health hospitals and clinics and the UCLA Psychology Clinic School. Her experiences are international and multicultural – including countries in Africa, Europe, the Caribbean, Mexico, Brazil, and India. She studies indigenous healing with renowned teachers from American Indian, African, and other traditions. She bundles this knowledge and passes it on to youth, emerging elders, and others seeking to fulfill a higher level of their potential.

11

THE BELOVED COMMUNITY: A MENTAL HEALTH PERSPECTIVE

By Sulonda Smith

What would our communities be like if pain and suffering did not exist? By trade, I am a psychotherapist, a mental health professional, so I have thought about this question often. I treat hundreds of people who suffer from abuse, misuse, and self-defeating behaviors. At times, pain and suffering seem like unavoidable conditions of the human experience. Some people believe suffering is a choice and that we can change our emotional settings.

My perspective is that we choose *when* we want to shift our emotional awareness and expressions. In our community as a whole, whether local or global, we can choose to heal ourselves beyond the emotional "overwhelm." First, we must choose to heal ourselves, and become aware that the task is a delicate dance of consciousness. Then we can help others in our community remember that they too can heal. Consequently, our communities will harness the collective energies of our expressions of joy, peace, love, abundance, and prosperity.

Healing oneself is not as attainable a goal for someone who has been taught, and therefore believes, that pain is more real than happiness. Our intuition, or inner knowing, and subtle signs help guide our human journey. Sometimes we forget that we have our own built-in navigation systems, or we just do not know we have a direct line to the Source of all answers. When people look outside themselves for answers, which is something I encounter often in therapeutic sessions, as well as in my own life, they are distracted from their awareness that they have a certain level of control over their own life. When people become aware of their personal power, and take ownership of beliefs, thoughts, and actions, they can begin to heal from various traumas. Sometimes it takes a professional, or a mother, or even a loving friend to initiate this healing process.

The connection we have between us as a human family is the responsibility of accountability for each other's wellbeing. For us in a social society, our daily interactions weave together like a Persian rug, from the person who builds our homes to the person who employs us. Having courage and vulnerability allows someone to help you survive and thrive. That is an act of reciprocity, as one gives and the other receives. We are not here alone. "I got your back even if you can't have mine in the moment" is a philosophy that we can adopt as we practice unconditional love and compassion. True blessings do not come by giving with the expectation of receiving in return. Blessings come from giving and knowing that you have already received in the blessings of those people and things that bring you joy, contentment, and happiness. Our pool of appreciation is wide and attainable within the community.

Community is such a precious gift because the expression of self mirrors in each encounter, whether with a tree, a cat, or our grandparents. We are all invaluable gifts. We have tremendous value and offer great service to one another. One simple service can be offering a smile to someone familiar or unfamiliar. Research in western psychology has shown that it is easier for a person to be unhappy and negative than it is to be happy and fulfilled. Have we accepted this practice of negativity within our communities and society? We may have subconsciously embraced this way of expressing ourselves.

Many traditional healers around the globe say that our natural state of being is luminosity–*the state of awareness of being light in the mind, body and spirit; a celestial being.* Perhaps instead of trading ill will, adversity, or hatred, we can barter abundance, loving self-expressions, and unconditional love. When we offer a healthy reflection to one another, all aspects of our lives can shift positively. As a consequence, no one hungers, wars are forgotten, and cares for our brothers and sisters across the planet spread like wildfire.

To conclude, I remember and honor the fires that bring people together to tell their story of existence. To marvel at our similarities with others over distant lands and to practice reciprocity with one another and Mother Earth is healing medicine. It is to all relations that we honor others and ourselves. Whether two-legged, four-legged, six-legged, winged, rooted, seen, or unseen, we share this home. Whether from a western psychological perspective or from indigenous knowledge, thriving in the pursuit of right relationship is paramount to healing oneself, one's brother and sister, and one's beloved community.

Sulonda Smith was born and raised in Milwaukee, Wisconsin, and now resides in Atlanta, Georgia. As a psychotherapist and traditional arts practitioner, she imparts delicate tools essential for maintaining healthy and loving relationships. Sulonda is a licensed professional counselor, coach, consultant, live event facilitator, and radio/TV presenter.

12

GROWING UP ON THE WEST SIDE OF BALTIMORE

By Carl Rubin

I can remember as a young boy, maybe 8 to 10 years old, being at 2900 Garrison Boulevard on the West Side of Baltimore City. It was there I gained an informal education about life. You see, my grandfather and grandmother had moved to Baltimore from South Carolina. My grandfather worked two jobs at a time to obtain a better future for his beloved family. He had a vision, a desire, and, more importantly, he had a PURPOSE!! 2900 Garrison Boulevard was the address of my grandparents' laundromat, located on the corner, at the bus stop across from, at that time, a 7- Eleven and several small shops that lined the street from Duvall Avenue to Grantley Avenue. My grandmother ran the show. She was the one everybody called "Mama", from Jim Parker's cut-rate store to the Walbrook Junction. Mama Davis was a name as common as the nightly news anchors on Channel 13! Mama Davis would be there when someone needed to have a hot meal or needed some clothes for their children. She was everybody's mama in those blocks and beyond!

I can't help looking back and connecting how my grandmother was a source of happiness, comfort, and love for so many. It was ritualistic how people would come to the laundromat to feel the love and nurturing from Mama. What a woman. But none of what she did would have been possible without her man, my Pop, who had the vision and the desire to develop a business that would be for our people in our community. He worked diligently to obtain his vision. He had PURPOSE!

If we travel down the 2900 block of Garrison Boulevard today, we can see how the landscape has, indeed, changed. The laundromat no longer exists; it is a vacant lot. The 7-Eleven is now a convenience store owned by Middle Easterners. The apartments that took up the upper part of the block have been sold and renovated by a foreign investment firm. The majority of the people who now occupy the neighborhood are renters and not business owners. We have lost the "Mama Davises" and the "Pops"--mom & pop shops– which gives me cause to question: Has our increase in consumption crippled our desire or will to be producers?

This is what I now see happening around me: broken families are the norm in today's morally loose, gender reversed society. Mama now plays the role of Pop. Are we not even aware of the traditional roles of male and female, husband and wife, mother and father, son and daughter, yin and yang? Our harmonizing (hormones) energy is being disrupted; and, unifying family values we used to hold dear have been forgotten while other nationalities that hold family and gender roles sacred are the new business owners in our communities. Are our visions only centered on the trivial pursuit of consistent and immediate consumerism, instead of an overall focus on strong family, strong community, and an even stronger nation?

We must *overstand* what the roles of the traditional, natural nurturer and provider are, i.e., female/male. If a woman (mother) has to assume the role of the man (father), her feminine energy turns into provider, masculine energy, and, thus, detracts from her natural, feminine, nurturing energy. The absence of strong willed innovative men has forced our beautiful mothers and sisters to assume this provider (masculine) energy or position. Being the all-loving nurturer, she may take on this role unaware of the deep, ethereal damage this is causing her and her children.

As a result of this role reversal, I see children gaining a distorted perspective of gender roles and gender identification, thus, causing numerous unfavorable situations that we, as a nation, are burdened with today. A very troubling concern in the Black community is the lack of fathers in the home. As a result, our young men are running wild with no course of direction. I recall a study conducted on young male adolescent elephants that would terrorize the community and fight weaker elephants, causing all kinds of damage when the elder male elephants were absent. But once the elder male elephants were reintroduced into the community, all of the misbehaving stopped immediately! Even in the animal kingdom, gender roles must be obeyed or destruction is not far behind. It is time for the elder males to reintroduce themselves to the community and give the much needed guidance and instructions to our young men.

One may ask, have our young men lost PURPOSE? Perhaps it is simply that they have no elder males present to guide or discipline them. Perhaps they see the woman being the provider of the family and doing the work we, men, by nature are commissioned to do. Perhaps many young men feel hopeless because they have no income or skill sets to provide for a family, and this causes an internal quarrel that is then externally expressed in the ways they communicate with our sisters by calling them hoes and bitches, etc. Some sisters view these males as disrespectful, incompetent, and unsuitable to be fathers or lovers. Many sisters feel they can raise children without these men and the negativity they bring. What a big and tangled web we are in!

As a 34-year old man with African DNA, I cannot help but be connected to the Universe, because I am a universe! I am a mirror of the outward Universe we all occupy. Indeed, there is a great necessity, an almost innate calling, for a man to have a clear, decisive PURPOSE, and to cultivate a burning desire to fulfill that PURPOSE for the good of the Universe, not only for self-fulfillment, but also in accordance with the harmony of the Universe.

So when this balance is compromised, of course, it affects me; and, I hurt with my universal family. My immediate family has suffered many of the ills that plague society today (drugs, broken families, loss of income, cancer, etc.). I have been told that in order to know your future, you only need to look at your past. My ancestors are close to me no matter how far I travel away from Source. They speak to me, call me back, and tell me, "Look at what your grandparents have done, what they have provided for you." They remind me of this whenever I see someone who says, "I miss Mama Davis. She was like a mother to me." Or they will say, "Pop was a hard working man that built an empire through vision and PURPOSE."

My beloved Mama, my sisters, my love, our nurturer, the mother who comforts and gives unconditional love! We cannot disconnect from her, or this source of Mother Love! We need and must have it to accomplish our masculine PURPOSE. For we, as men, live at our greatest potential when we are defending, protecting, and serving this motherly essence. Brothers, this is our PURPOSE---to be a rock of determination, and to never give up providing and protecting our mothers, sisters, and wives.

As of today, I feel that men with African DNA in my community are struggling with this ancient concept, and have no understanding of this sacred PURPOSE. This disconnect is a reality for so many of our brothers. I can only imagine what our women are going through. It has to be much worse because the female energy receptors as very keen; and, she is more emotional and sensitive to energy imbalances than the masculine energy. We, as a universe, are going through some turbulence, to say the least! My inherent connection to the Universe and Source is attracting the resources and strength to carry out this divine PURPOSE!

Brothers, fathers, and sons, it is time for us to reconnect to our PURPOSE and to cultivate the burning desire to defend and honor our mothers, sisters, and wives. It is our masculine duty to serve her and to protect her love, so that she can continue to nurture the planet. When we rise to that innate purpose, that instinctive drive that every man possesses, this planet will operate at the level of its true divine purpose and provide all of its inhabitants with infinite LOVE. What a time to be. Our disconnect is only as far away as our ability to connect back to our divine PURPOSE. Let's get to work family!

Carl Rubin (aka Caruben) was born in Baltimore Maryland. His poetry is featured in several anthologies, published by Eber & Wein. He is proud father to Chevayo Amaru. As an actor, Caruben starred in The Image entertainment release "For Thy Love" (2005). Caruben is also a hip hop artist (VeganG) who's smash hit R.O.M.E (Rule Over Men Everywhere) can be downloaded from iTunes, Amazon music, Google Play, Spotify, and many other digital music outlets. Caruben is the founder of Putdownthemeat.com, an online blog dedicated to all things Vegan. You can follow him on Twitter: @putdownthemeat

13

THE SCENT OF A PLACE

(Portions of this essay appeared online for the San Diego Free Press)
By Will Falk

I often wonder why I write. 100 species went extinct yesterday, 100 species will go extinct today, and 100 more will go extinct tomorrow. One in three women are the victims of sexual abuse worldwide. Every mother has dioxin – a known carcinogen – in her breast milk. Dioxin poisons the most intimate human connection, the connection between mother and child.

I volunteer with the Vancouver Island Community Forest Action Network. This morning I told the director of the organization that I would not be in the office today until well past noon. When she asked me why, I simply said, "Writing." She rolled her eyes and sighed.

The world is burning, and I sit in a coffee shop with pen, notebook, and laptop to write?

In the last two years, I've tried to kill myself twice.

There's never a simple answer for suicide. I was a young trial attorney in the State of Wisconsin's Office of the Public Defender. I was exhausted working 70 and 80-hour weeks trying to be the best attorney I

65

could be. I was gripped by despair as it became increaseingly apparent that I was nothing more than a rubber stamp for a criminal justice system where 95% of cases end in a guilty plea, where, as Michelle Alexander says in *The New Jim Crow: Mass Incarceration in the Age of Colorblindness*, there are more black men imprisoned today than were enslaved in 1850.

Worse than all of this, though, I lost a sense of enchantment with the natural world. My friend, environmental writer Derrick Jensen, once wrote, "We have a need for enchantment that is as deep and devoted as our need for food and water." I learned that this is true after isolating myself in my office, in jails and prisons around Wisconsin, and then in the weak, electric light of my apartment in Milwaukee, poring over case files at 3 AM night after night after night. With no time to remember my proper place as a humble member of a natural community, I began to see the world as a fundamentally dreary, dead place where humans with power controlled humans (and everyone else) without power.

This culminated in a severe case of depression. Twice, I buckled under the weight of it all. Twice, I poured pills on a counter top, ground a few into powder with a butter knife, snorted the pills up, and downed the rest with a glass of water.

It's been over a year since my last suicide attempt, and I've been learning how to keep my demons at bay. The first step to recovery was forgiving myself for developing the despair that engulfed me. I've heard that despair is a natural reaction to a desperate situation. And, I know that living in a world where some scientists question the ability of the human race to survive the next half-century that we truly occupy a desperate situation. I have learned that I am not crazy for feeling the despair I feel. I am not crazy; I am merely alive.

I've also learned that despair is simply an emotion and no emotion, no matter how deeply felt, can kill me. I can kill me. I can put a gun to my temple, I can run a hose from the exhaust pipe into the cab of a car, or I can swallow too many pills. In each case, though, it takes a physical action to kill me. Sitting with my despair, however, by itself, cannot kill me. Taking this idea further, if it takes a physical action to kill me, it also takes physical actions to pull myself from the darkness of despair.

Because my despair is the result of the direness of the environmental situation and my loss of connection to the natural world, I have built a road to recovery on actions to protect the environment and tangible steps to recovering my sense of enchantment with life.

In my analysis, climate change is the scariest environmental concern we face. We know that the burning of fossil fuels is most responsible for climate change, so if we want to stop climate change we must stop burning fossil fuels. In May 2014, I left the

United States to volunteer at the Unist'ot'en Camp, an indigenous cultural center and pipeline blockade in so-called British Columbia, Canada.

Lead by Unist'ot'en spokeswoman Freda Huson and her husband, Toghestiy, the Unist'ot'en Camp sits on the traditional and unceded territory of the Unist'ot'en Clan of the Wet'suwet'en First Nation. "Unceded" means the Unist'ot'en never signed a treaty, sold their land, or lost a war to the Canadian state. The territory, in every sense, is and always has been the Unist'ot'en's. Right now, the territory is threatened by a number of proposed pipelines that would carry fossil fuels from the tar sands gigaproject at Fort McMurray, Alberta across Unist'ot'en land, on the way to processing facilities in Kitimat, BC, to be shipped to markets worldwide.

The Unist'ot'en refuse to allow any pipeline to cross their territory, so they've built physical structures on the precise GPS coordinates of the proposed pipelines routes. A traditional pithouse blocks one pipeline, a cabin blocks another, a bunkhouse stands in the way of a third, and a permaculture garden was constructed on the path of a fourth proposed pipeline route. Currently, there are plans in the works to build a wellness center and healing lodge to support indigenous mental health.

We have all signed our share of petitions, voted for candidates we think will do the least amount of damage to the environment, and hoped and prayed that the destruction will cease. The Unist'ot'en, however, are putting their bodies directly in the path of forces that are destroying the world. Volunteering at the Unist'ot'en Camp has given me a chance to alleviate my despair by acting in physical defense of the environment.

The question still remains, though. While there is work to be done at the Unist'ot'en Camp, while physical forces are destroying the world, why am I sitting in this coffee shop writing?

I just returned from a winter visit to the Camp. A snowstorm arrived a day before we did, dropping over a foot of snow and stillness on the territory. The clouds cleared the second night we were there, opening the skies to the silent music played by the twinkling of countless stars. While most of the crew sat around the wood stove in the cabin a hundred yards away, I stood sniffing the air around me.

I was thinking about a conversation I had with Toghestiy about poetry earlier that morning. I explained that writing poetry is my passion. I told him I wasn't sure why exactly, but poetry helps me make sense of things. In his quiet, serious way, Toghestiy smiled, watched the smoke from the wood stove cling to the corners of the cabin, and said, "A good poet gives you the scent of a place."

It wasn't until I was lucky enough to walk his trapline a few days later that I understood what he meant. And, what he meant is why I write. At Unist'ot'en Camp, the trapline is a trail where traps are set for martens, fishers, beavers, and wolverines. Walking the trapline means snowmobiling out into the bitter cold and then snowshoeing several miles, checking each trap for animals. Toghestiy was raised culturally and he remembers how to space his traps so that no population of animals is overburdened. The furs of these animals bring in money to support the blockade. Walking the trapline is an ancient tradition honored by generations of indigenous trappers, and is filled with connection to the past.

My friend and I rounded the last corner of the trapline about a quarter mile from the snowmobile ride back to the cabin. My feet were frozen, my hips were cramping, and I was hungry when my friend elbowed me and pointed to the trees ahead of us. The sun was setting behind a wall of pines. The pine needles in the branches facing us were cloaked in silver shadows while the sun threw a blanket of gold on everything else. The snow scattered the light like the stars I watched a few nights before. Next to me, the tracks of a grouse twisted over a snow bank before disappearing with no trace but the faint outline of wings brushing the powder.

I heard my heart pumping blood through my eardrums. I heard trees dropping snow in piles. I heard my friend breathing softly. I heard everything praying. In my backpack, I could smell the fermented salmon eggs we used as bait for martens and fishers. I also carried a syrup jar containing a purple mixture of beaver castor, anise oil, glycerin, and raspberry jam we spread on trees as lure.

In short, I heard and smelled enchantment. And then I remembered: Life is really good. I want to live. I want all of this to live.

Sitting in this coffee shop, attempting to express what I learned, I know, now, why I write. I write because many are not lucky enough to experience the scent of places like the Unist'ot'en Camp in the ways I have. I write because many are starving for the enchantment that humans need so desperately. Writing, by itself, will not save anything.

But, a good poet recognizes and reveals the ways the land gives all meaning. A good poet gives you the scent of a place. And, once you have the scent of a place, how can you fail to protect it.

Will Falk moved to the West Coast from Milwaukee, WI where he was a public defender. His first passion is poetry, and his work is an effort to record the way the land is speaking. He feels the largest and most pressing issue confronting us today is the destruction of natural communities. He is currently involved in support work for the Unist'ot'en Camp – a pipeline blockade and indigenous cultural center situated on the Unist'ot'en Clan of the Wet'suwet'en people's unceded territories in so-called British Columbia. His work regularly appears online for the San Diego Free Press.

14

WHY THERAPY ON A FARM?
THE JOURNEY TO JENLO FARM
By Lois Hickman

There were my father's nightly bedtime stories about 'Grampa' Turtle or 'Grampa' Catfish who warned the little boy who'd gone fishing not to hurt their babies, shortcuts through the woods on my way home from school where I picked wild strawberries and violets, witnessed snakes digesting mice, and nearly lost my boots in the sticky springtime mud; angry tears and sign-wielding protest marches over a maple tree being cut down, or a vacant lot—our softball field—being desecrated by construction of a new house.

There were regular pilgrimages to my grandparents' farm in Shepherd Michigan. The potatoes and beets, cabbage, onions and carrots harvested there were stored in their root cellar. Ah, the musty, earthy smell of that root cellar! Peas, beans, apples, plums, tomatoes, and berries grown on our 1/8 of an acre in Flint, and the grapes and peaches bought from local farmers, joined the Shepherd produce in rows of shining glass jars under the attic stairway, and constituted most of our winter fare.

Living within minutes of aunts, uncles and cousins on a "poor folks" dirt road just outside the Flint city limits, it was often difficult to tell which child belonged in which household. The depression and family calamities created a need for everyone taking care of each other. You never knew which cousin's feet would be on your pillow. It all depended on who needed to be taken care of. The trailer in the back yard belonged to an out-of-work family friend who also happened to be a poet. He was part of the family for five years. Community.

Leap forward many years. With an Occupational Therapy degree on my wall, and a profession to call my own, the influences of those early years became evident. At Boulder Community Hospital, treks on the greenbelt land outside the hospital grounds were easily woven into therapy sessions. At The Children's Hospital in Denver, I worked with a social worker and a speech therapist to develop an 'outward bound' camp experience, in Breckenridge, Colorado, for children with sensory integration disorders. In our clinic in Niwot, Colorado, we hiked on a trail where families of owls graced the ancient cottonwoods. We visited the goat farm, only a mile away, sometimes to enjoy hot cocoa, with a stream of goat milk squirted directly into a mug of instant cocoa mix. Ah, delicious!

At Stonebridge Farm near Lyons Colorado, we began yearly summer camps for children with special needs. And finally, with the purchase of JenLo Farm (directly west of Stonebridge), therapy for children and adults is blended into the real work of caring for rabbits, pigs, goats, chickens, ducks, fish, dogs, cats, and at various times, a Jersey cow, a miniature horse, and even a turkey who had fallen off the truck to the processing plant at Thanksgiving time. Farm therapy addresses all the issues that are usually thought to belong in a clinic, but without the feel of a hospital or clinic.

It's a caring community. Kids don't like to leave; they feel almost as if this farm belongs to them, as they learn where the feed is kept, what kind of care each animal needs, and how, as the seasons change, the needs on the farm change. They develop a respect for life and a love for the natural world. Going beyond the farm, clients often are part of visiting the local hardware or feed store, or going to Steamboat Mountain Natural Food Store where scraps are saved for the animals. Community awareness and inclusion broadens the influence of therapy on the farm.

Our farm community has expanded to include friends from around the world. In addition to the many occupational Therapy students from the United States who have had internships here, there have been outstanding students from Japan and Ireland. After his internship at JenLo, Daniel Fitzgibbon planned to develop his own private practice on his family's farm near Tipperary. Occupational and physical therapy students and professors from Japan come for regular tours, to experience the uniqueness of therapy on a farm and to explore ways they might take this close-to-the-ground philosophy into their own practices. Our community has become global.

The environment suits me well. I live where I work. I have a place where I and other therapists can practice Occupational Therapy in a natural setting. At the end of the day, there may be feet on my pillow, but now instead of cousins they're apt to be a dog, a cat, a crippled chicken, or even a duck. There are stories to tell. It's a good life.

Lois Hickman, MS, OTR, FAOTA In her over 40 year career as an occupational therapist, Lois Hickman has become internationally known for her innovative work with children and adults with special needs. Music, story, interaction with animals, and the earth are woven into therapy on her small farm in the foothills of northern Colorado. She knows how critical it is that this connection to nature be fostered; and, it is her joy to be able to provide a place for this to happen.

Part Four
JUSTICE

15

RESTORATIVE JUSTICE
(*From Oakland Tribune 'My Word'*)
By Fania E. Davis

The third week of November was Restorative Justice Week. Oakland officially declared it in 2011, joining celebrations worldwide. We've seen amazing successes in the past years in advancing restorative justice approaches in schools and the juvenile justice system. Oakland has a lot to celebrate.

Restorative Justice for Oakland Youth launched California's first urban school-based restorative justice pilot at a middle school in 2007, reducing suspension rates by 87 percent, eradicating violence and teacher attrition, and improving academic outcomes. These successes led the school board to adopt restorative justice as official policy in 2010.

Today, restorative justice is in almost 30 Oakland schools, with a growing infrastructure of staff at the district and school site levels. At a current RJOY pilot, a last-chance continuation high school, graduation rates are up and violence, suspensions, and racial disparities in discipline have been eliminated.

According to a school district report soon to be released, from 2011-2014, suspensions of African-

American students for defiance decreased by 40 percent; harm was repaired in 70 percent of conflict circles; students are learning to talk instead of fight through differences at home and at school; and graduation rates and test scores are increasing while chronic absence and dropout rates are decreasing.

Oakland is also trailblazing restorative juvenile justice practices. Inspired by the successes of New Zealand's Maori-influenced Family Group Conferencing, Oakland's Community Works West has launched a restorative diversion pilot that is dramatically reducing recidivism.

The Oakland-based National Council on Crime and Delinquency is helping other jurisdictions initiate similar pilots. Insight Prison Project is launching an in-custody restorative program. RJOY is pioneering a restorative re-entry model. The North Oakland Restorative Justice Council paints murals, plants trees, and facilitates healing circles after youth homicides.

Residents and police are working together to keep children out of prison. Police, probation officers, youth and others are being trained in restorative justice. Youth and police are sitting together in healing circles, creating new relationships based on increased trust and recognition of one another's humanity. Given the epidemic of police killings the nation is now grappling with, our work with law enforcement offers hope.

This year, RJOY kicked off Restorative Justice Week with a daylong gathering to celebrate the indigenous roots of restorative justice. We watered the roots so that the tree of restorative justice might continue to flourish.

Indigenous elders from North American, South American, African, and Asian traditions gathered at Lake Merritt Park, facilitating ceremonies on the land for peace and healing, and engaging in intergenerational conversation with the children.

Diverse communities celebrated together with intercultural food, dancing, singing, storytelling, and drumming. The children are learning that the shift to an ethos of peace, healing, and community that restorative justice invites is deeply embedded in who they are.

Our traumatized communities, especially the children, need this kind of ancestral medicine for sustenance and healing. Oakland is emerging as a national model in using cultural restorative justice approaches to interrupt the school-to-prison pipeline, break cycles of racialized mass incarceration, and bring community healing.

Our successes are receiving national media attention from The New York Times, NPR, NBC, PRI, Smithsonian Institution's Story Corps, and others. The feds have taken notice. Civil Rights Assistant Secretary Russlyn Ali noted what is happening in

Oakland is "a model process we hope to see repeated again and again across the country."

Fania E. Davis *is co-founder and executive director of Restorative Justice for Oakland Youth. For more information, visit http://rjoyoakland.org.*

16

THE RESPONSIBILITY OF LEADERSHIP

By Sekou Cinque T.M. Kambui

To liberate ourselves we must be willing to do whatever is necessary (by any means necessary) to eradicate ignorance and mis-education, to *overstand* every condition of our lives that hinders our success and prosperity (our enjoyment of a better quality of life) for ourselves and our children.

We must make a stand:

- To eradicate ignorance and mis-education;

- To overcome injustice, poor quality healthcare;

- To eliminate poor quality housing and dilapidated, impoverished neighborhoods;

- To *overstand* criminalization of our youth & the accompanying mass incarceration of them;

- To eradicate our addictions that cripple us and undermine our potential for success and total and absolute liberation;

- To respect and love ourselves, our Leader(s) in all we do;

- To embrace, unconditionally, our commitment to the total and absolute liberation of us as a people;

- To Love Ourselves and Each Other;

- To learn the importance of showing respect for ourselves and others;

- To learn and *overstand* there is, there should be, only (for each other) ***ONE LOVE!!!***

In my early years as a youth coming up in the 50's and 60's Civil Rights / Black Power Movement(s), I was drawn to, and became affiliated with, several groups because of their diversity of ideology and philosophy, such as cultural nationalism / Pan Africanism, revolutionary nationalism, and such, like the flavor of militancy brought to the forefront by the working class people that you and I have come to know as our fathers and mothers, our sisters and brothers, our neighbors even. Their militancy, too, in many forms, demanded major structural changes in the realities we faced (and continue to face) as a people; we, who have forever been denied, deprived, even divested of full citizenship and rights in this country. Local, state, or federal agencies moved brutally and decisively to repress the growing radical youth of my era. THUS, COINTELPRO.

In our world, we, victims of the Willie Lynch Syndrome, (*have been subject to*) Amerikanism, i.e. forced assimilation/adoption of, or acculturation into, a euro-centric concept of life, philosophy, political ideology, economic dependency, and social hegemony, where we hold ourselves in check out of misplaced respect for/fear of 'WHITE SUPREMACY', and a self-negation of our own importance to world affairs.

Specifically, you and I are besieged by dysfunctional family life: one parent homes, where, most of the time, the mother is compelled to attempt to raise a man-child to manhood without a father figure to mold and shape the pattern she elects for his life. She's a likely victim of un/under-employment, drug / alcohol addiction(s), even mental health issues from a traumatized life of child-abuse that she, herself, was coerced to suffer in silence, even denial. She likely struggles with menial or low-paid work for lack of adequate education to qualify for better work conditions. The deliberate dismantling of the normal social safety net – the father or husband's assistance in such matters – absent, due to criminalization in the popular media, and increased police violence, the objective being to promote, condone, and manufacture into existence the "RATES OF INCARCERATION OF OUR MEN, WOMEN, AND OUR YOUTH" and introducing into our midst: "MASS INCAR-CERATION".

Therefore, you who profess yourselves to be leaders, who desire to be respected as leaders, or you are leader(s) in your particular area of interest or expertise, whether as a politician, a political/civil/human rights activist/leader, a leader of a chosen religious community (denominations or declaration of faith is irrelevant here), a leader of one Youth Organization or another, **MUST,** in assuming the role as such a leader, be cognizant of the responsibilities that attach itself to your role as "LEADER."

As a leader, whether religious, secular, social, political, or cultural, you have a responsibility to those whom you are chosen to or called to lead; to take historical stock of the present political, economic, and social landscapes. The state of things in your home with your families, your wives, and children; and whether the condition you and I are in is the best possible condition it can or should be for us; we must also be aware of and know who is in control of how things are for us, in our lives, in our homes, and in our communities, and whether those in control – if not we ourselves – are making and acting on decisions made with our best interest in mind, or with the objective being for you and I to be successful and prosperous, and in good, proper, and necessary mental, spiritual, and physical health.

Our New Afrikan (Black) Youth are, still, poorer than most other demographic groups, with over 50% living below the poverty line. Our New Afrikan (Black) Youth are more likely residing in dysfunctional, dilapidated, deteriorating poverty-stricken homes and neighborhoods. Thus, you and I, and our youth of every era, have been left with the elements of survival that is (was) easily criminalized, and thereby, as a result, "you and I" must now come together to realize that our potential to overcome the indignity and injustice of our situation or predicament lies within the hearts and minds of our Leaders in our world today.

In your era, which my era now overlaps, disaffected New Afrikan Youth, like many of you, with most radical organizations no longer on the scene (of your communities—because of police violence and murder or COINTELPRO arranged incarceration), your energies have been found expressed through your involvement with the more negative influences in our world. Youth Organizations like the Bloods, and Crips, GD's or BGD's, Vice Lords, New Black Panther Party, the Nation of Gods and Earths, the Moor(s) vie for attention to renew focus of our youth on more positive, uplifting things to bring into manifestation, and introduce and secure a better world for you, me, US!

This being said, our newly formed Leaders(s), adopted Leader(s), or those whose sacrifices in the struggle for a better quality of life, gave birth to them as Leaders, or Political Prisoner(s), even Prisoner(s) of War, have a responsibility to us as a people, to our youth, whatever their status in the world around us, to demonstrate Leadership qualities and characteristics, that reflect the love they have for us as a people, and whose everyday sacrifices in our name and on our behalf, earn our respect, adoration, admiration, and, by example, show us/teach us how to liberate ourselves.

Sekou Cinque T.M. Kambui was formerly incarcerated for 47 years, wrongly convicted for a crime he didn't commit. He has been part of the Black Liberation Army, Black Panther Party, Student Non-violent Coordinating Committee (SNCC), Congress of Racial Equality, Inmates For Action, Atmore-Holman Collective, Social Consciousness Development Group, Cultural Awareness Think Tank (CATT), New Afrikan-PP (Political Prisoners), and POW (Prisoners Of War).

17

LEONARD PELTIER
By Geri Timmons

Leonard Peltier, Native American AIM (American Indian Movement) Activist, has been languishing in a United States federal prison since 1976 for a crime he did not commit. His case is considered one of the greatest travesties in modern judicial history; the trial is widely recognized as a miscarriage of justice. Former Congressman Don Edwards, longtime chairman of the House Judiciary Subcommittee on Civil and Constitutional Rights, former FBI agent himself, and a strong supporter of clemency for Peltier, wrote on December 14, 2000: "Even the government now admits that the theory it presented against Mr. Peltier at trial was not true. After 24 years in prison, Leonard Peltier has served an inordinate amount of time and deserves the right to consideration of his clemency request on the facts and the merits."

In January 2014 the United Nations Special Rapporteur on the rights of indigenous peoples, James Anaya, met with Leonard Peltier at the federal penitentiary located in Coleman, Florida where Mr. Peltier is incarcerated. In recognizing the need for reconciliation with the country's indigenous people, Anaya stated to the United Nations: "This should include efforts to identify and heal particular sources of open wounds that they continue to experience, including new or renewed consideration for clemency for Leonard Peltier."

Amnesty International, in a statement released on February 10, 2014, highlighted the following areas of concern in relation to Mr. Peltier's case:

- Questions about evidence linking Leonard Peltier to the shootings;
- Coercion of an alleged eye-witness who said she had seen Leonard Peltier shoot the two agents, but who later retracted her testimony, and who was not allowed to be called as a defense witness at Leonard Peltier's trial; and
- The withholding of evidence by the prosecution at trial, including potentially key ballistics evidence, which might have assisted Leonard Peltier's defense.

Amnesty International is urging the US authorities to release Leonard Peltier from prison in the interests of justice and on humanitarian grounds. Leonard is now in his thirty-ninth year in captivity, and is in failing health.

Mr. Peltier has spent the years of his struggle for freedom productively initiating humanitarian projects such as the Leonard Peltier Healthcare Reform Package, Native American Business Enterprises (a program to stimulate Reservation-based economics and investments), and the establishing of a scholarship at NYU for Native American students seeking law degrees. In March of 2010, Peltier organized an art benefit on behalf of the victims of the earthquake in Haiti. Every year he sponsors a gift drive for the children of the Pine Ridge Reservation. Leonard Peltier is widely recognized for his humanitarian work, receiving a variety of awards. He has been nominated for the Nobel Peace Prize six times; he is also an accomplished artist and writer. Mr. Peltier has garnered substantial international support from people in all walks of life to include, but not limited to: National Congress of American Indians, many Nobel Laureates, scholars, legal professionals, Foreign Parliaments and Commissions, literary artists, musicians, celebrities, and civil rights leaders.

The struggle for Leonard Peltier's freedom has not stopped; Mr. Peltier is preparing to once again ask the President of the United States to grant him executive clemency. The ILPDC continue in their efforts to build mass support for Leonard Peltier's freedom. He only has one option left, one hope remaining and that is President Obama.

For more information or to join the campaign please visit the website at www.whoisleonardpeltier.info or call 1 (302) 310-1575.

Geri Timmons has been a grassroots organizer and political activist working with the International Leonard Peltier Defense Committee for over 20 years and has known Leonard Peltier for approximately 41 years. She was living on the Pine Ridge Indian Reservation at the time during the Reign of Terror.

18

WHAT GOOD IS TALKING IF NOBODY'S LISTENING?

How truth telling and dialogue can help heal the wounds of structural racism in a post–Ferguson America

By Tony Jenkins

The U.S. justice system's non-indictment of the officers who killed Michael Brown and Eric Garner has illuminated the structural racism inherent in our culture and institutions. This racism has been with us all along, but the string of obvious injustices, very publicly revealed and discussed in the wake of the deaths of two young black men in America by police officers, has jump-started a movement that demands a new model of justice and wholesale social and cultural transformation.

To say a nerve has been touched is an understatement. There has been a swelling of intense pain and frustration in Black America for a long time. Emotions can be turbulent when triggering events reveal to the oppressed that their very life has been an experience of daily injustice, and the heightened conversation confirms the intuition that something has been wrong all along. Eric Garner, suspected of selling "loose cigarettes", died when New York police placed him in a chokehold and sat on his chest.

In these moments, talking doesn't feel like action; and, the urge to be civil is tempered by observations of an uncivil system. U.S. political culture models a very ill-mannered form of discourse in which politicians talk past one another, making it impossible to work toward the common good.

"Speaking truth to power" accomplishes little or nothing when nobody is listening – including those who are speaking. I believe that activists engaged in this movement aren't so much tired of talking; they are skeptical with just cause. However, truth-telling and dialogue still have very real promise in shaping a more preferred future and healing some of these wounds.

Developing faith in public reason and the mechanisms of dialogue takes time, but it may be the most effective way of bringing about social change and changing the fabric of race relations in America.

One of the reasons for our new found consciousness around race is that structural racism is insidious and, for the most part, invisible. From the end of the Civil Rights era until the present moment, it has not remained elevated in our cultural narrative. That's the nature of structural racism and structural violence: they are so deeply codified into the norms of our culture and the tenets of our legal system that they seem innate.

Those in privileged positions don't even notice it, as their biases of the culture have no bearing on their day-to-day lives. This is privilege blindness. This isn't the case for young black men in America who have a very real and reasonable fear of the police. This is supported by the oft cited ProPublica report that finds young black men are shot dead by police at a rate 21 times greater than that of young white men, and the Pew Research Center's finding that black men are six times more likely to be incarcerated than white men.

The NAACP has a fact sheet on racial disparities in incarceration rates that sheds light on the systemic nature of the problem. Amongst the facts they highlight is an analysis provided by Unlocking America suggesting that if "African American and Hispanics were incarcerated at the same rates of whites, today's prison and jail populations would decline by approximately 50%."

How Transformation Begins

These invisible patterns of injustice, accompanied by the very visible shooting death of Michael Brown and the choking death of Eric Garner, bring awareness to a social problem that has laid dormant or otherwise ignored by the privileged that define the parameters of mainstream culture.

In transformative learning theory, these are the catalysts or trigger events that shock and shake up our worldview, and cause us to question our reality. As pioneered in theory and practice by the recently deceased Jack Mezirow, transformative learning with adults seeks to bring about changes in perspective that will guide future action. Mezirow described ten phases of transformative learning that is distilled into four more basic stages: a triggering event, critical reflection, rational discourse, and action.

The trigger event, described by Mezirow as a disorienting dilemma, is not transformative in and of itself. Trigger events can lead to many outcomes, even reinforcing past attitudes. Transformative outcomes generally depend upon the quality of opportunities to process or to engage in critical reflection on the experience. This is a critical step in questioning our assumptions about how the world is and operates.

The protest stage of a movement, generally emerging quickly after the trigger event, can provide a collective space for transitioning to critical reflection. While protests on their own rarely produce lasting change, they are a vital part of the change process. The general media perception of protests is that they serve only as a space for elevating an issue, the collective expression of shared anger, and, in some instances, the non-violent disruption of the status quo.

Yes – protests can lead to violence; such is always the possibility when emotions run high and participants encounter the threat of a highly militarized police force. However, as David Ragland, a leader of a truth-telling campaign in Ferguson, reflects, protests play a role in building community and for collectively helping make sense of the triggering experience.

Ragland suggests, "Protest in general is important for dramatization of issues. It's important for solidarity, networking, understanding the issues, and making yourself part of a public forum."

While a well-organized protest can provide a space for critical reflection, this is rarely enough. Intentional opportunities for internal and community reflection on the issues need to be provided. Further critical reflection must also have an internal and external component.

The external dimension requires observation and analysis of the systems of which we are a part. In the context of justice, it requires questioning how the rules of society were created, by whom, and for whom. The internal dimension is more challenging, demanding us to confront and challenge our assumptions about our role in the problem and to be open to changing our self. This is a step that is difficult to reach without the support of an intentional community of practice.

Critical reflection can also build empathy and help us to consider the context of the other. The reflections of NFL player Benjamin Watson in response to Ferguson, posted and virally spread on Facebook, are a great demonstration of empathic critical reflection. I encourage you to read his reflections in their entirety.

Here is one of Watson's most poignant introspections: "I'M INTROSPECTIVE, because sometimes I want to take 'our' side without looking at the facts in situations like these. Sometimes I feel like it's us against them. Sometimes I'm just as prejudiced as people I point fingers at. And that's not right. How can I look at white skin and make assumptions but not want assumptions made about me? That's not right."

Acknowledging our biases and their origins aids in perspective taking and in framing the issue with reason. This is a humanizing process that moves us past positionality, and opens us to the possibility of actually hearing one another. Getting to this state of reciprocity demonstrated in Watson's reflections is a necessary prerequisite for engaging in rational discourse, the next phase in Mezirow's architecture of transformative learning.

This is particularly relevant in the context of the political relationships that are inherent in a public forum. Parties engaged in public discourse need to agree to present and listen to reasonable arguments.

Dialogue is a particularly transformative form of discourse. Harold Saunders, President of the International Institute for Sustained Dialogue, describes its transformative nature: "Dialogue is a process of genuine interaction through which human beings listen to each other deeply enough to be changed by what they learn. Each makes a serious effort to take others' concerns into her or his own picture, even when disagreement persists. No participant gives up her or his identity, but each recognizes enough of the other's valid human claims that he or she will act differently toward the other."

It is easy to see how critical reflection and rational discourse are necessary prerequisites to engaging in this form of transformative dialogue. To be able to listen, to truly hear and learn from one another, requires this preparatory reflection and thought work. This form of dialogue is very distinct from the polarizing culture of political discourse. It is oriented toward the common good; emphasizes healing and building the relationship rather than solving the issue; and encourages participants to listen and not speak past one another.

Truth-telling and Dialogue in Action

How might truth-telling and dialogue, as transformative processes for healing the wounds of structural racism, appear in action? In the past few weeks there have been some public calls for the establishment of a truth-and-reconciliation commission on race in the United States. Truth-and-reconciliation commissions have had success around the world, most notably in addressing apartheid in South Africa.

A coalition of groups on the ground, led by the Center for Educational Equity and the Peace and Justice Studies Association, is establishing a "National Community Institute for Truth, Justice, and

Reconciliation in Ferguson & Beyond." A truth-telling project will kick off soon to collect personal stories of people of color victimized by police violence and other forms of institutionalized racism and injustice.

Speaking truth is important. At a political level, it's a way of documenting injustices and making them public. Truth-telling is essentially a form of critically reflective storytelling, and as personal narrative it humanizes the social dilemma by rooting it in human experience.

The International Institute for Sustained Dialogue (IISD) incorporates story telling as a critical and transformative dimension of its approach. Through assessment of several of IISD's sustained dialogue efforts, Philip Stewart and Nissa Shamsi observe how story telling can build empathy: "In Sustained Dialogue, [as seen in examples cited in their research], when differences or conflict are seen as identity-based, participants are encouraged to relate their personal stories. Often these involve various kinds of traumatic experiences with people like others in the dialogue. These stories often invoke cognitive (I understand where you are coming from) and then emotional (I feel what you are feeling) empathy for the story teller, resulting, over time, in a broadened sense of identity capable of accepting, at one end of response, and of embracing at the other."

With this understanding, truth-telling/story-telling

can be viewed as a necessary bridging process, transforming parties in a dialogue from adversaries to fellow humans connected in a complex, interrelated web of experience that each has interpreted differently based upon relative positions of power and privilege, culture and worldview.

The dialogue that follows truth-telling can be transformational if the conditions of openness, empathy and public reason are present and agreed upon. Getting to this stage can be the hardest part. There are many modes and practices of dialogue, each suitable to different contexts and requiring various levels of preparation, skills, and experience.

The National Coalition for Dialogue and Deliberation offers a beginners guide to dialogue work and provides details for over 180 tools and methods for public participation. Restorative justice (RJ) is a particularly relevant dialogue model for the exploration of structural racism and justice. Based on indigenous circle processes, RJ emphasizes a conception of justice that holds community wholeness and integrity at its core. If the proper conditions are met and principles adhered to, most dialogue models have the potential to be transformative.

Inching Toward Social Healing

Action, the final stage in Mezirow's transformative learning model, actualizes the transformative process. For the individual, action equates with behavioral and attitudinal change and the development of transformative capacities rooted in empathy, perspective taking, and listening skills.

At the social and political level, transformative action requires relationship building supporting cultural change; the modeling and testing of new social institutions and democratic practices; and experimentation with new processes of justice that have human dignity at their core.

From an emotional vantage, such as that experienced at early stages of the transformative process, this may seem like an inconceivable level of action and change. History, however, reminds us that fostering the long view is essential. The preferred order may not emerge entirely in our lifetime, but we may cultivate the conditions and cultural qualities for enduring change for future generations.

Healing the wounds of structural racism in a post-Ferguson American through truth-telling and transformational dialogue is a challenge we must accept. The deaths of Michael Brown and Eric Garner have triggered an awakening of consciousness, which through intentional opportunities such as the "National Community Institute for Truth, Justice, and Reconciliation in Ferguson & Beyond" may lead to the critical reflection essential for perspective taking and new meaning making.

Through dialogue, new ideas and perspectives on racial justice can be confirmed, in and by community, and just relationships can be built that may lead to action for sustaining change through ongoing engagement and fostering new ways of being together.

Tony Jenkins is the Director of the Peace Education Initiative at the Judith Herb College of Education at The University of Toledo, OH. He also serves as the Managing Director of the International Institute on Peace Education and Coordinator of the Global Campaign for Peace Education, and is a member of the UNESCO Experts Advisory Group on Global Citizenship Education. Most recently, Tony was the Vice President for Academic Affairs at the National Peace Academy, and prior to that, the Co-Director of the Peace Education Center at Teachers College, Columbia University.

Part Five

HONORING
DIFFERENCE

19

I AM

By Tori Wolfe-Sisson

I am. The words that follow that statement can only describe what I may appear to be. This is important because those adjectives can place me in or kick me out of communities.

Human, woman, Black, and lesbian are the identifiers that sculpt the experiences illuminating the perspective I speak through. It is often assumed that I am a straight woman, and that sometimes can unfortunately serve to separate me from members of the lesbian, gay, bisexual, transgender, and queer community. With a less than confrontational physical appearance, it is with ease that others categorize me without my input. Sometimes, while in academic communities and circles that seek solutions for issues in Black communities, an unspoken prerequisite is that I leave my *same gender loving identity* at the door.

The way we interchange thoughts and opinions by speech, writing, or signs begs us to call upon our individual memories and experiences to identify what is placed before us. Because we live in a society that is dominated by European centered thought that has been generally cultivated by older, straight, white men, we must be cognizant of how we convey information. While discussing the LGBTQ community and relationships, it is vital that we understand appropriate language. During the long battle for marriage equality in the United States, the term "same-sex couple" became a household term to describe LGBTQ couples. There is issue with this terminology because it highlights the sexual aspect of relationship in contrast to "straight couple" where that merely describes a relationship between two opposite gender individuals.

Audre Lorde once said that poetry forms the quality of light from which we predicate our hopes and dreams toward survival and change, first into language, then into idea, then into more tangible action; and, it has also been said that gender is the language we use to live our poetry to the world. Sandwiched between the oppressive forces of racism, classism, homophobia, sexism, and ostracism, it has been a task to define the *Beloved Community* in relation to the LGBT Community- or lack thereof. Utilizing the term "community" serves to make speech easier when describing the peoples within it; however, the accuracy wanes when those individuals do not feel that sense of community.

Martin Luther King Jr.'s vision of the *Beloved Community*, while it could be described as a form of democratic socialism- it did not aim for the inclusion of same gender loving individuals within the general community. Bayard Rustin was a phenomenal civil rights strategist who is remembered as the organizer of the 1963 March on Washington; he brought Gandhi's protest techniques to the American civil rights movement and helped mold Martin Luther King Jr. into an international symbol of peace. When Rustin was arrested on a "morals charge" in Pasadena, California, it changed the approach to his activism in a drastic way. Rustin was silenced, beaten, arrested, imprisoned, and fired from important leadership positions, largely because he was an openly gay man in a vigorously homophobic time.

Although we currently reside in an era of inequality and minimal justice, it seems we have yet to overcome intersecting issues. In an already divided community, attempts at working toward solidarity through political action serve to divide the community in ways that are ironically not supportive. Although the queer community shares a rejection of the definition of "traditional sexuality" and "traditional family," structure, race, class, ableism, national origin, marital status, veteran status, citizenship, and gender identification/perceived gender does not cultivate camaraderie.

"When a people share a common oppression, certain kinds of skills and joint defenses are developed. And if you survive, you survive because those skills and defenses have worked. When you come into conflict over other existing differences, there is a vulnerability to each other which is desperate and very deep," enunciates Audre Lorde's observation surrounding the crossroads of intersection and the dire need to work through it. Of the divisions in the queer community, the forces come from factors, including religion, visibility/lack thereof, pressure to conform to societal norms, and attempts to live out a heteronormative lifestyle, that does not coincide with their truth.

As for my experience as a feminine identified, Black, lesbian woman, I realize that I have found safety in over sexualizing myself. Out of a fear of corrective rape, I have exuded confidence lent to me by lies of sexual conquest. Deriving from a heterocentric belief in machismo competition, I have been unfaithful to women to validate my membership in this community against the stereotypes around feminine identification. My femininity felt weakened in contrast to the strength of masculinity- and so I found myself painting a persona for the world that did not include my authentic self. With the walls I built to protect myself from the world, I now have to work to get to know myself without barriers. I have forgotten my honest views of fidelity, ignored the more genuinely liberated modesty of my spirit, and I must reconsider how I share myself.

It is, in part, by identifying a craving for community while addressing the flaws in places we meet discomfort that I hope to propel us forward. In first disassembling the gender binary and its divide among folks who fight for recognition of gender neutrality, it seems we are the answer. We must exemplify respect and solidarity, but how? We must be ever present in the understanding of our human condition. If we were equal, we would have no reason to fight and it cannot only be police brutality that unites us. There is something about us all that makes us "unfit" for "first class citizenship" in America. As long as we come from a place of compassionate understanding of the common ground on which we walk- we can call ourselves community without having to bleed out our humanity.

People with same-sex desires have existed throughout history. What has varied is the way society has viewed them, and how the people we now describe as LGBT regarded themselves at different stages. In society at large, the penalties for homosexuality have historically been severe. State laws across the country criminalized same-sex acts, while simple affectionate acts in public such as two men or women holding hands could lead to arrest. Even declaring oneself as a gay man or lesbian could result in admission to a mental institution without a hearing. June 28, 1969 in New York's Greenwich Village an unremarkable event sparked a flame that has began to light the way to liberation for the LGBT community. Around 3 am, seven plain-clothes detectives and a uniformed officer entered a gay bar and announced their presence.

The bar staff stopped serving the watered-down, overpriced drinks, while their bosses removed the cigar boxes that functioned as registers. The officers demanded identification papers from the customers and then escorted them outside, throwing some into a waiting paddy-wagon, and pushing others off the sidewalk. This was nothing out of the ordinary, but on this particular late night/early morning bust, the people were sick and tired of being sick and tired, so they fought back. Hundreds of gay men, lesbians women, trans, and cisgendered people (black, white, Hispanic, and predominantly working class) converged on the Christopher Street area around the Stonewall Inn to join the fray. The Tactical Patrol Force would disperse the jeering mob only to have it re-form behind them, yelling taunts, tossing bottles, and bricks, setting fires in trash cans. In the wake of the riots, intense discussions took place in the city's gay community. During the first week of July, a small group of lesbians and gay men started talking about establishing a new organization called the Gay Liberation Front. The name was chosen for its association with the anti-imperialist struggles in Vietnam and Algeria.

Movements organized to propel racial equity used the term "Black Power" to express a range of political goals, from defense against racial oppression, to the establishment of social institutions and a self-sufficient economy. The efforts of the Black Nationalists and similar groups were thwarted by the existence of COINTELPRO. Gay rights organizations were targets during this time period, as were all other groups that did not adhere to the ideology promulgated by J. Edgar Hoover, who was himself a closeted "sexual deviant" by his own definition. The purpose of his new counterintelligence endeavor (COINTELPRO) was to expose, disrupt, misdirect, discredit, or otherwise neutralize the activities of black nationalist "hate-type" organizations and groups, their leadership, spokesmen, membership, and supporters. Hoover's goals were to expose the background of groups, and expose their personal lives and organizational conflicts to public scrutiny where such publicity has had a neutralizing effect.

Similarly to the current plight of the Black community, the LGBTQ community has been lulled into complacency by the appearance of safety and protection. With a little help from the media and the fact that accurate information must be thoroughly researched, it seems like our global issues are unrelated. When the transgender community is attacked, the general population does not feel affected, when the gay community is attacked, the straight community does not feel affected, when the brown community is attacked, Black and white communities do not feel affected; when the Black community is attacked, we look to their socioeconomic status to determine if its just.

What!? Now take notice, what about when a Black transwoman is assaulted? What population is concerned about her screams? When genocides are constructed by political establishments, peoples across the globe are passively concerned, yet in their own front yards don't we cry out for international outrage? In which tax bracket must one reside for an assault to be either justified or absurd? Is there a sexual orientation or gender identity that allows one to maneuver about the world safely? If so, why is that and is that fair? We are one body of humanity; and, if any one of us lives in fear that our lives may be extinguished by someone else's hate, we are all unsafe.

Currently, the national climate has been described as "open season on Black men," notes Rev Denise Donnell, who goes on to observe that "open season" on queer and transwomen of color has been largely ignored. It has been too long that we have ignored our intersectional realities and not been intentionally strategic in working as comrades toward solution. The Combahee River Collective states, "we are actively committed to struggling against racial, sexual, heterosexual, and class oppression, and see as our particular task the development of integrated analysis and practice based upon the fact that the major systems of oppression are interlocking. The synthesis of these oppressions creates the conditions of our lives." Neither of our intertwined communities has done a good job, as a whole, of being aware of our sociopolitical and economic power to support of cease to support businesses/organizations based on their support for us as a whole.

We see larger corporate social justice advocacy organizations releasing guides for how to shop with businesses supporting LGBT equality; however, we do not have any of these guides on a larger scale for businesses who have fair trade, socially and environmentally responsible business practices. It seems that in our quest to change the status quo, we have proven our lack of respect for the system as a whole and that may be more detrimental than we realize. There are models of organizing individuals, events, and groups that have been created by corporate structures that would help to unify our movements; however, for the simple fact that a system has been created by a corporate structure, we sometimes deny its usefulness, and that is problematic.

While Martin preached integration- I only agree with that model of unification while it is intentional in preserving the authenticity of communities and cultures with respect to the outside world. If we are to eradicate the separation and self-segregation of Black/brown and white queer community, we must continue to be respectful of the authenticity of our cultures and allow them to flourish uninterrupted through our communion. With the intention of intersection in regards to so many different yet very connected issues, we need to look to our examples of appropriation among diverse communities and work to preserve cultural integrity as we learn from each other in liberation.

In large part, the Black church experience serves as one of religious of dissent and affirming church culture. This church culture glorifies the one-dimensional existence of their edutainment ministerial community, i.e. Gay choir directors and ministers, praise/liturgical dancers, and/or bible study warriors who, out of fear of rejection and eternal hellfire, only permit one facet of themselves to exist in the walls of the church. You will notice that this chapter sites very few numbers, because how can any study be valid when it would require the participants to be open and honest and when jobs, families, friends and God is at stake- the people willing to participate skews the data. For people who have grown up in the Black church, or even for persons who have dropped in for a service or two, this is a common experience. The closet culture breeds psychological, emotional and physical ailments due to stress on multiple levels. These individuals consistently attend services that speak to their deepest fears and offer only the solution of working to change their honest same gender attraction into a forced opposite gender relationship that should lead to "holy matrimony".

As a people who have been beaten down and oppressed on an international scale for roughly 500 years, it is clear to see that one population is now working to use their slight acceptance in mainstream America to prove themselves as "normal" in oppressing another minority population. In regards to women, Audre Lord says "the oppression of women knows no ethical nor racial boundaries, true, but that does not mean it is identical within those boundaries;" and, that almost perfectly articulates the funny thing about working as a being who is oppressed consistently, because of the unique existence as an intersection of inequality.

In appropriating the skill and creative genius of any one or all of these members of the edutainment ministerial community, the church benefits from the skill, while the community member suffers at the hands of the message that is sent when gay bashing sermons are taught, female submission is instructed, and/or when immigration is explained in a way that promotes are not helping the nation or the economy.

My vision of community includes healthy non-discrimination ordinances that include immigration status, national origin, sexual orientation, gender identity, and veteran status along with the 1964 Civil Rights Act to protect folks from discrimination by giving them a means to report incidents that would be legally dealt with. This vision also includes community gardening, cooperative economics, as well as supplemental education programs thus enriching smaller communities and providing solutions to some of the issues surrounding poverty and this country's wealth gap. I understand that a healthy community looks vastly different to each individual who imagines it, but in opening the community to deliberately dialogue around issues that affect us, it allows growth and perpetual development.

The next steps to cultivate the Beloved Community in the LGBTQ community and throughout the communities LBTGQ people intersect starts with introspection and honesty. I wonder how it might shake some people up to really begin to admit the flaws in previous methods of organizing, as well as some of the bigotry of marginalized minorities against others. When faced with facts around something one believes to be real that dismantle that reality can be harsh and scary to confront. As we look inside ourselves and encourage speech that is not derogatory towards any group of people, realizing our roles in acting out microaggressions that breathe life into discrimination and, ultimately, hold our individual selves accountable for the society we have taken part in creating, *then* we are on the path to creating change.

I am a firm believer in the notion that one should look inside to solve problems before placing blame, because in our own ways, and in our most insignificant actions, we often find that we have not led by example 100% of the time to model the ideal society we desire. In naming my vision and ticking off these simple bubble gum steps to creating significant change, I understand that it appears to be bigger than that and readers will likely call this model flawed. It might be flawed, but the matters are not all that complex. Living beings need water, food, shelter, love, and security. Beginning with spaces like the "projects" of the inner cities that are clear signs of a failed project, cooperative economics alongside barter systems as well as the other specifics outlined in my vision previously can become embedded into the structure that receives members of the community who are both moving in and currently living there. With proven models of efficiency in the microcosm of a project- the structure can be replicated and tweaked to be culturally competent in diverse spaces.

My point is ultimately, that there is a sense of community; however in reality that community is disjointed so severely that one may argue that it does not exist. We must work in unison to be the Beloved Community that we articulate ourselves to be members of.

Tori Wolfe-Sisson is a bold young woman, viewing art and activism as the perfect way to affect the human condition toward justice. Like a gust of wind from the "battle born" state, she moved from Las Vegas, Nevada to Tuskegee, Alabama, "pride of the swift growing south", stopping in Texas on the way. Choosing to live and work in Alabama, she and her wife, Shanté Wolfe-Sisson have committed to be the change they wish to see by living openly and sustainably. They feel that it is of the utmost importance to be accessible to young people and able to answer as many of their queries as possible because they both understand the struggle of being young, Black, lesbians who are "out" in the rural South. In accepting the role as a community organizer, she finds joy in empowering a population with information that will help them live comfortably – information is the best weapon to fight injustice.

20

WHEN DISABILITY IS THE DIFFERENCE AND THE BELOVED COMMUNITY

By Janora Ware

"But the end is reconciliation; the end is redemption; the end is the creation of the beloved community. It is this type of spirit and this type of love that can transform opposers into friends. The type of love that I stress here is not eros, a sort of esthetic or romantic love; not philia, a sort of reciprocal love between personal friends; but it is agape which is understanding good will for all men. It is an overflowing love which seeks nothing in return. It is the love of God working in the lives of men. This is the love that may well be the salvation of our civilization." *From "The Role of the Church in Facing the Nation's Chief Moral Dilemma" - 1957*

"If you're so perfect, how come your Momma walks with a cane?" A braided nine-year old delivered a blow to my daughter, Jazzelle, a fellow fourth grader in the bus line at the end of a very long school day. The stinging words hurled at Jazzelle hit her chest with a force, and sunk deeply into her heart. This mean girl had used her words to paint a photographic image of the pink elephant in our life at the time. She came home from school with the corners of her mouth sloping downward, nearly dragging her milk chocolate brown face on the floor. Her eyes glistened with tears as she explained that she had been teased in the bus lane by another brown-skinned classmate about my disability.

In my thirteenth year of living with Multiple Sclerosis, we experienced a severe decline in health. I use "we" because even though the symptoms affect my physical state, the disease affects my entire family. It was a challenging year engaged in a life altering struggle to battle the most severe progression of MS in my body, since my diagnosis in 2001. The relapse began shortly after the kids had started school in September. The MS had made its debut at the local school in November, as I visited my daughter's cake pop stand on Young Entrepreneurs Day with a hickory carved cane for support. The image of me slowly and awkwardly walking through the fourth grader's various businesses was the image that stuck in that young girl's mind. It is an image she would use as a tool of destruction.

I looked at my daughter and thought about the other girl. I couldn't see my daughter ever saying anything like that because she has a heart of acceptance and tolerance. She developed this over time growing up with a Mom who, herself, struggled with disability and various degrees of physical limitation. My heart was hurt for my daughter; I never wanted her to be ostracized or excluded because of me. My heart also hurt for the other girl who had the self-loathing energy to destroy another through the use of differences as a weapon. It saddened me that she likely wasn't taught or had not the experience to know any better. My gut reaction was to go up to the school with my cane and tell her it's for bopping disrespectful kids. Then a surge of compassion filled me as I said a silent prayer for that girl and her single mother. Jazzelle did what felt right in her heart; she walked away from the irate girl, and came home to be immersed in love.

To myself and other disabled community members, unconditional love of humanity in all its forms, including "thyself", is essential nourishment to the healing process. By the end of that school year, I was rolling through my summer days in a wheelchair I named Lucy. Disability is like skin tones; it is arbitrarily random and often extraordinary. It takes a beloved community to see the value in differences, of gender, of abilities, of religion and of skin tones. Collectively through the unharnessed and relentless spirit of Agape love, we can nurture a healing beginning in our own bodies and spread it throughout those around us. Just like people, healing doesn't come standard; but, it comes subtly when encouraged and filled with faith. Martin Luther King, Jr. had a vision of tolerance, acceptance, and unconditional love to create beloved community – A community where people aren't afraid to look at you because they don't want to stare at your disability; A community where children are taught to see the beautiful person behind the difference, and set the example for the future.

Janora Ware, a.k.a. J.Kharma, graduated magna cum laude as an honors scholar from Kennesaw State University with a B.S. in Integrative Studies. The integrated fields of concentration of her specialized degree combined foreign language, professional writing, and film studies. She is currently near completion of her MFA in Creative Writing at Southern New Hampshire University. As a recipient of the Clendenin Fellowship, she is able to fund her lifelong passion of storytelling. Recent accomplishments include publication in an anthology entitled "Letters to Friends: Wisdom Through Storytelling" and production of a short film screenplay entitled "40 Steps". Her screenwriting portfolio includes a feature film, a short film, and an original Atlanta-based "pilot."

21

THE VISION OF A WORLD FOR ALL

By Shariff Abdullah

(Adapted from the award-winning book, "Creating a World That Works for All")

Where there is no vision, the people perish.
– Proverbs 29:18 The Bible (King James Version)

We live in a society lacking a coherent, inclusive vision. Vision and goal setting are important: without a clear vision and an achievable goal, along with an understanding of the philosophy and values behind that goal, we run the risk of becoming sidetracked, confused, burned out, or cynical.

The Essence of Inclusivity

Simply put, our inclusive vision is *an inclusive human society on a habitable planet*; a society that works for all humans and for all nonhumans. This means fulfillment both for those who are at the top of the society and for those at the bottom. Work, resources, responsibilities, spiritual gifts, and material goods may not be evenly spread, but everyone has "enough"; anyone could trade places with anyone else without feeling deprived or oppressed. Such a society is essentially benign and healing to both the human and the more-than-human world.

All beings, all things, are One. Our lives are inextricably linked one to another. Because of this, we cannot wage war against anything or anyone without waging war against ourselves. Therefore, we are obliged to treat all beings the way *we* want to be treated. There are no "enemies"—all beings are expressions of the Sacred, and must be treated as such. Some beings cause pain to others; this does not mean that they are enemies. Some beings are food for others; this is all the more reason to treat them as sacred. Once we understand that we are interconnected, we have the responsibility to create a world that works for all.

With this as our goal, the next question is obvious: how do we achieve it? How do we avoid sinking into despair or cynicism? And how do we avoid dabbling in utopian fantasies or engaging in "pie-in-the-sky" religiosity? In fact, we can change this world right now by shifting our consciousness and our values from a foundation of exclusivity to one of inclusivity.

This shift in consciousness is the core of the world's major religions and wisdom traditions. The essence of the moral code they urge upon us is inclusivity.

What is hateful to you, do not do to others. - Rabbi Hillel

*Do not hurt others with that which hurts yourself. -
Buddha*

*Do unto others whatever you would have them do unto
you. - Jesus*

*None of you is a believer until you love for your neighbor
what you love for yourself. - Muhammad*

Considering the clarity, simplicity, and consistency of
these statements, one has to wonder what it is about
the message of inclusivity that makes it nearly
impossible for people to either comprehend or
implement. Why are there Jews, Buddhists, Christians,
Muslims, and many others around the world who are
killing their fellow men and women when their
traditions call for peace, nonviolence, and inclusivity?
We must face these questions if we are to pull our
society back from the brink upon which it now stands.

A Turning Point
Do you feel the promise in these perilous times?
Despite our many challenges, do these times feel
hopeful to you in some way? Does it seem to you that
something is ready to change? How are we going to
capture the promise that lies within our present
predicament as we stand on the brink of the twenty-
first century?

The hard fact is that getting to a world that works for
all will take a more rigorous analysis and more
sophisticated actions, both internal and external, than

our current political, social, and even spiritual leaders are advocating. It will take fundamental change that must originate with *you*, as an emerging leader of the new millennium. The old theories (capitalism, communism, anarchy, progressivism, conservatism… even democracy) are incapable of delivering a world that works for all. If our current leadership were capable of it, they would have done it by now.

Such change does not take place at the surface, but deep within. It is already at work. We are all a part of it. The ice breaking on a frozen river is an indication of warming trends and currents that have been at work for a long time. The breakup at the surface is the culmination of a process, not it's beginning. The breakup of ice on a river, the emergence of a butterfly from its chrysalis, a Declaration of Independence, each culminates a process that has preceded it by days or decades.

Prerequisites of Change

One of the mistakes many of us made in the Sixties was thinking we all just had to love each other and the evil system would go away. Despite our good intentions and hard work, we did not understand the processes of societal change. And, we were at the mercy of those who did understand.

Systemic change does not miraculously bubble up from a change of heart. It is intentional, stemming from a precise and rigorous examination of present conditions and an understanding of the consciousness and spirit from which those conditions have emerged.

When Karl Marx analyzed capitalism, he did so with the same consciousness that created capitalism in the first place. Marx, as a Breaker scientist, saw an "I am separate" world, a world of limited resources, a world in dire need of human domination and control. This is what his consciousness was trained to see, and the system of communism was built upon that consciousness. He and Friedrich Engels inspired the creation of a political structure controlled by a small elite, an industrial empire that ecologically devastated the land, sea, and air in its never-ending quest for more resources. The system created by Marx's disciples Lenin and Stalin killed, jailed, tortured, and oppressed tens of millions while being blind to its own contradictions or the aspirations of its people.

Communism was merely another manifestation of Breaker consciousness. What looked like a different system was only a different way of looking at the same system. Marx analyzed the conditions but not the consciousness. Same wine in a slightly different bottle.

What Is Exclusivity?

Exclusivity is the notion that "I" am separate from "you" (or any "Other"). This notion is what Einstein called a *"delusion of consciousness"*, a delusion that imprisons us. No beings other than humans suffer this delusion. And not all humans see themselves as separated entities. Indigenous people see themselves as an integral part of their local ecology, making the notion of selling land as absurd to them as selling parts of their bodies.

In itself, exclusivity is not bad; the problem is being imprisoned in this myopic way of viewing self and world. Separation becomes a *delusion of consciousness* when you believe it's the only consciousness that's possible. A surgeon operates on her patient from an "I am separate" perspective, having the objectivity to cut open and manipulate the patient's body. From the patient's point of view, objectivity is a good thing.

Exclusivity is the root of all of our human maladies. ALL OF THEM. It allows us not only to separate from others but also to oppress them. Racism, sexism, terrorism, homophobia, slavery, torture, all forms of hatred and bigotry, stem from the notion "I am separate from you—by virtue of skin color, ethnicity, behavior, belief . . ." It is exclusivity that allows a bomber to kill unarmed civilians— whether a suicide bomber on a bus in Sri Lanka or an Air Force bomber dropping an atomic weapon on a city. Of the 110 million deaths from wars in the 20th Century, two-thirds of them, 73 million, have been of civilians. For the proponents of exclusivity, this has been a very active century.

According to the theory of exclusivity, a society that works for all is impossible. Not "difficult" or "challenging" – completely impossible, like throwing a ball and hitting the Moon. The Breaker story holds that a restructuring of our priorities and our consciousness is impossible. The status quo is called "human nature."

Massively Reinforced Delusion

Everything we have learned in formal education and in our culture reinforces the notion that the world can work for only a few. History, anthropology, psychology, politics, economics—and our fathers and mothers—strengthen the idea that the world cannot work for all.

Think back to your first economics course. On the first day, the teacher or professor said something like, "Economics is the allocation of limited resources." You didn't question it, you dutifully wrote it down—it fit your world picture. That laid the groundwork for all the later explanations of why some were millionaires while others were permanently unemployed.

Both winners and losers tend to believe that the world is limited and can work only for a few. Those on the bottom seek to make someone else lose rather than questioning the assumptions built into the system.

As Menders, we believe that an inclusive society is not only possible but is achievable *right now*, with the resources presently available to us. We don't have to wait for more resources or better technology. For example, we know that every year, America produces enough grain to feed every hungry person in the world, and has the means to distribute it. We do not need more technological advances (or more GMOs) to feed starving people; we need a change of heart that leads to changes in our priorities and systems.

A world that works for all is *not* achievable without restructuring our priorities, our attitudes, and our culture. We cannot tinker with this... the change must be fundamental—an evolutionary shift toward spiritual compassion, and corresponding shifts in our actions. In short, **a transformation of head, heart, and hand.**

We must work on ourselves first, and then be prepared to do the work on our culture and institutions. The essence of this work is spiritual, a trans-religious quest for the reality that transcends our ordinary experience.

"Another world is not only possible, she is on her way. On a quiet day, I can hear her breathing." - Arundhati Roy

Dr. Shariff Abdullah is an author, consultant, and a leading catalyst for inclusive social, cultural, and spiritual transformation. He is an expert in the field of societal transformation and in the emerging field of "demos-dynamics" – how human populations interact and change. He is the founder and president of Commonway Institute and the originator of the Commons Café and the Common Society Movement. Sharif is the recipient of many awards, and his peace-making work with Sarvodaya Shramadana contributed to the 2002 historic cease-fire in the war in Sri Lanka. His books include "The Power of One: Authentic Leadership in Turbulent Times" and the award-winning "Creating a World That Works for All."

22

A COLLEGE TEACHER'S EXPERIENCE OF BELOVED COMMUNITY

By L. Nef'fahtiti Partlow Myrick

I am relatively new to teaching college and still too much in love with my work and students to be discouraged by the politics of academia, or whatever it is that burns some teachers out while sucking the passion out of others. Being an almost-full-time adjunct faculty member from a nontraditional career track probably helps. I came to this work a 50-something artist-writer, peace walker, and spiritual activist after years of working in community and having seen what is possible when people create a space for other people to realize oneness, respect, love, healing, and humanity. I bring this practice to every English composition and literature class I teach, and am constantly amazed by the outcome. Constantly.

My approach to teaching begins with the realization that students are, first, *people* with varied interests, experiences, perspectives, and attitudes that affect how they show up in the undefined community that is a classroom. They show up for obvious reasons—a grade, to learn, to get a degree—but most often, at least at the community college where I teach, they show up for reasons beyond the obvious. Whatever the case, I recognize that each person has said YES to going forward in her/his life. This is no small thing; and, I honor that choice. My challenge is figuring out how to engage and retain all these different people, with all their dreams and baggage and stuff, in an academic experience that will serve them in and beyond the classroom.

The paradox is that they must be accountable and responsible for designing their own learning experience. While my role is to teach and facilitate a learning experience through which they obtain certain levels of competency and mastery in course objectives, it is ultimately up to them to establish the context for their experience. In other words, they must have a vision for what they want and the desire to make it happen. Such is the nature of college and every student's role.

So my first, day-one question to every class I teach is this: *If you could have a meaningful, ideal learning experience, what would that look like? What will it take to make you want to show up for every class? What do you value?* Students then work in small groups to answer those questions, and to begin the process of consciously creating the experience they want. Sometimes they do not get what they have done until the end of the course; possessing the power to create your own reality is a strange concept to them. Yet, this assignment never fails to empower students with a sense of ownership in their class while laying the foundation for the community they will become, rooted in a culture of shared values, openness, and trust.

My job is simple after that: create assignments and activities that are relevant to both the individual student and community; hold classes as a sacred space; and treat classrooms as ceremonial grounds. I have witnessed real human magic when students KNOW they are in a safe place to be who they are—Latino, black, white, gay, straight, Muslim, Christian, Wiccan, wealthy, homeless. When they feel accepted, when they are free to express genuine compassion, and when they are courageous enough to tell their truth, "even when it's not pretty." When they can cry if they have to and laugh when necessary. I have also seen the most resistant, insecure and learning-challenged students flourish in this learning environment upon gaining skills they did not dare imagine they could possess. This is the power of the Beloved Community in action.

This is where I want to live all the time.

Like many teachers, I consider my work a sacred service. To contribute to another person's growth and development on their path to becoming something bigger/brighter/better is a privilege. This is why I love my work, which never feels like a job, and why I keep falling in love with students from one semester to the next.

Lenett Neffahtiti Partlow-Myrick is a visual artist, poet-writer, senior adjunct English instructor at Howard Community College, and instructor for Goucher College's Educational Opportunity Program. She taught performing arts, poetry, and life skills development for over 35 years, and has worked as a technical writer, editor, and publications designer. She has held writing residencies with the Ripken Reading Center, Liberty Medical Center, Baltimore Homeless Union, and Miami Light Project. Her poetry has appeared in numerous publications, and her visual artworks have been exhibited in solo and group shows. Her innovative work as a performance poet has been captured in the award-winning video documentary Mbele Ache and the CSN-TV special "Voices of Our Past." Lenett was named one of HCC's inspiring adjunct faculty members for 2013-2014.

23

INDIGENOUS CALL FOR URGENT, UNPRECEDENTED, AND UNIFIED ACTION FOR PROTECTING AND RESTORING THE SACRED

By Hereditary Chief Phil Lane, Jr.

The spiritual foundation of this Call for Urgent, Unprecedented, and Unified Action is based in the understanding of the fundamental oneness and unity of all life. Clearly, as well, all members of the Human Family are all part of the Sacred Circle of Life. Since we are all part of the Sacred Circle of Life, we are all Indigenous Peoples of our Mother Earth. This makes every Human Being responsible for the wellbeing of one another, and for all living things upon our Mother Earth.

Therefore, whether or not the nation states, multinational corporations, or international development agencies that surround us are willing or able to participate with us at this time, it is clear our Indigenous Peoples and Allies are moving forward in rebuilding and reunifying the Americas and beyond, through the Natural Laws and Guiding Principles that are inherent in our Indigenous World View and Legal Order, rooted in an eternal and spiritual enduring foundation.

1. We have the ancient prophecies and the clear vision of a future of social justice and collective prosperity for the Americas and beyond that we are in the process of manifesting. This new global civilization that is unfolding, as promised by the Ancient Ones and the Ancient of Days, fully honors the Natural Laws and Rights of Mother Earth and the Unity and Diversity of Human Family. This New Spiritual Springtime foretold by our Elders is now unfolding globally, as surely as the sun rises every morning.

2. We have a strong, enduring and unbreakable spiritual foundation of cultural values and guiding principles that have empowered us to survive and arise, with greater strength and wisdom than ever, after a great spiritual wintertime. This long spiritual wintertime was filled, at times, with the utmost human cruelty, violence, injustice, abuse, and physical and cultural genocide.

Despite these challenges, throughout the Americas and around Mother Earth, our Indigenous Peoples are reawakening to their spiritual and cultural identities, and are healing our Sacred Relationships between ourselves, Mother Earth, and all members of the Human Family.

3. Together, with our other Indigenous Peoples and other Members of the Human Family, we have the cultural, spiritual, scientific, technological, social, environmental, economic, and agricultural capacities and wisdom needed to co-create and rebuild our Families, Tribes, and Nations stronger and more unified than ever before.

4. Our Indigenous Peoples of Mother Earth have the growing collective social and economic capital, coupled with vast natural resources, to bring our greatest dreams and visions to reality. This includes fully protecting, preserving, and restoring our Beloved Mother as the sacred heritage of all generations, yet to come!

Furthermore it is crystal clear that these collective resources are in the process of empowering us to become a primary spiritual and economic force, not only in the Americas, but throughout Mother Earth.

We are now and are destined in the future to play a greater and greater role as key global leaders in wisely mandating the sustainable and harmonious ways Mother Earth's gifts and resources will or will not be developed! We will insure that when the development of the natural resources of Mother Earth are not sustainable, no matter how much profit is to be made, they will not be developed!

Our Sacred Places and the Healthful Life of our Beloved Mother Earth are not for sale and exploitation for any price!

5. We, the Indigenous Peoples of the Eagle of the North (Canada and the U.S.) have the material resources to directly support our Indigenous Relatives of the Condor of the South (Latin America) in developing their collective resources, as they choose. The Condor of the South equally has critical resources to share with the Eagle of the North. Our greatest strength, yet to be fully realized, is our spiritual and cultural unity.

6. By utilizing emerging digital communications technologies and corresponding green technologies and economies, in harmony with our vast, collective social, economic, cultural, and spiritual capacities, we are manifesting, as promised, a future with social, environmental, and economic justice for all members of the Human Family and our Beloved Mother Earth!

7. The primary challenge that stands before us as Indigenous Peoples, and we, as a Human Family, in rebuilding the Americas, and beyond, is disunity. This disunity has been directly caused by genocide and colonialism. This genocide and colonization has resulted in unresolved inter-generational trauma and internalized oppression that is the process of being fully recognized and addressed.

As we move courageously and wisely forward, in greater and greater love, compassion, justice, and unity, we are reconnecting to our enduring and unbreakable spiritual and cultural foundation for healing, reconciliation and unprecedented, unified, compassionate action for "Protecting and Restoring the Sacred" everywhere on Mother Earth.

With the realization of this spiritual and cultural foundation for prayerful, wise, and unified action, all that is needed for our ultimate victory will gracefully and assuredly unfold at the right times and places, as foretold by our Ancient Ones.

With Warm and Loving Greetings,

Hereditary Chief Phil Lane Jr.,
Chairperson-Compassion Games International
and the Four Worlds International Institute

Chief Phil Lane, Jr. is an enrolled member of the Yankton Dakota and Chickasaw First Nations, and is an internationally recognized leader in human and community development. He was born at the Haskell Indian School in Lawrence, Kansas in 1944, where his mother and father met and attended school. During the past 44 years, he has worked with Indigenous peoples around the world. He served 16 years as Associate Professor and Founding Chairman of the Four Worlds International Institute, University of Lethbridge, Alberta, Canada. He has won numerous awards. In August, 1992, Phil was the first Indigenous person to win the prestigious Windstar Award, presented annually by the late John Denver and the Windstar Foundation to a global citizen whose personal and professional life exemplifies commitment to a global perspective, operates with awareness of the spiritual dimension of human existence and demonstrates concrete actions of the benefit for humans and all living systems of the Earth. At this event, in recognition of his lineage and longtime service to Indigenous peoples and the human family, Indigenous Elders from across North America recognized Phil as a Hereditary Chief through a Sacred Headdress Ceremony. He is a United Religions Initiative (URI) Global Trustee, representing North America.

Part Six
INTERFAITH

24

INTERFAITH IN THE DEEP SOUTH

By Reverend Glenda Davis

Our Interfaith Community here in Dothan, Alabama is a very important way for people of all faith paths to come together for discussion, study, and friendship. We are located in the southeast corner of the state, sometimes called 'The Bible Belt'. Traditionally, the South has demonstrated non-acceptance of differences among people – including racial, cultural, religious, sexual orientation and ethnic. The Interfaith Community is helping people become more educated and open to diversity. We've progressed since 1960 when John Kennedy, a Catholic, was elected President; and, there was an outrage among the predominately Protestant population in the South.

This Interfaith organization here was organized sometime since 9-11-2001 to help dispel the ignorance, fear, and negative emotions that were being demonstrated by some people. It was started in a progressive Presbyterian church, and has been regularly supported by people from various faiths – Protestant, Catholic, Jewish, Muslim, Hindu, Jainism, Buddhist and New Thought. There is still progress to be made, as some groups have chosen not to participate.

We have a monthly luncheon meeting, and also an Interfaith Thanksgiving Service that has been well attended the past 8 years. We soon learned that one thing people enjoyed about the Interfaith Thanksgiving Service was the reception following, with an opportunity to meet each other, comment on the topics and readings from the service, and taste some of the treats prepared from other cultures.

I think the primary benefit these gatherings afford us is communication, learning that at the heart we're really all the same. For the monthly meetings, we have chosen books to read, have attended lectures in the area, and viewed YouTube videos on various spiritual subjects, and discussed them in meetings that follow. What has resulted is a connection of the heart and lasting friendships.

I see gatherings like this as the only way to real peace and harmony between various religious cultures. As we learn more about each other, the walls of ignorance fall away and we are left feeling the joy of love that each one shines. We share news about our families, support each other in illnesses and losses and find a larger connection to the entire world through our connections with each other.

Rev. Glenda Davis is an inspirational teacher of the New Thought Centers for Spiritual Living (CSL) principles. Rev. Glenda has worked tirelessly for over 20 years with small groups and private individuals, supporting them in learning and using spiritual principles in their lives. At present, she is busy leading weekly Sunday services, facilitating Wednesday evening study groups, and teaching certificated classes. As of 2012, Rev. Glenda successfully taught and guided 7 new CSL students in becoming fully licensed CSL practitioners.

Rev. Glenda matriculated from Holmes Institute in St. Louis, Missouri, in 2003, with a Master's Degree in Consciousness Studies. In 2006, she was ordained as a CSL Minister and has been the Spiritual Director of the Spiritual Enrichment Center of Dothan for over 10 years. She also has an undergraduate degree in education and previously taught both elementary school and Montessori education. Rev. Glenda has also worked in banking, mortgage loans, and as a yoga teacher.

25

LOVE, COMPASSION, EMPATHY, AND PEACEBUILDING

The Rev. Victor H. Kazanjian, Jr.
(*Executive Director, United Religions Initiative*)

As Executive Director of the Untied Religions Initiative, a global grassroots interfaith organization working in 85 countries, it has been an extraordinary experience for me to travel the world witnessing acts of courage and daring carried out by people of different religious, and cultural groups working together to confront violence and injustice in their communities and build cultures of peace, justice, and healing for the Earth and all living beings.

What has struck me as particularly important about this work, and that of all movements dedicated to justice and peace, is that the power behind this peacebulding is less about politics and strategy than it is about relationship and human connection. After three decades of work as a community organizer, teacher of peace studies and grassroots activist, I have become convinced that without the power provided by love, compassion, and empathy, the most sophisticated strategies are but hollow branches bracing against the winds of injustice and violence.

Violence and injustice require the dehumanizing of the other. We know this – in both interpersonal and geopolitical contexts. Therefore, an essential component of all peacebuilding and justice-seeking is the rehumanizing power of love, compassion and empathy. We, who are dedicated to non-violent solutions to the world's problems, need to go beyond our familiar conversations about ending war and violence and establishing peace through merely instrumental means, and envision a new paradigm, an approach to peace that is about completeness, about wholeness within and without; a peace where strategies are based on the values of love, compassion, and empathy, and are rooted in the spiritual principles that ground our search for the Beloved Community.

Dr. Howard Thurman, mystic, poet, teacher and interfaith visionary speaks of this search in his book For the Inward Journey.

> *"There is a sense of wholeness at the core of humanity*
>   *that must abound in all we do;*
> *that marks with reverence our every step,*
> *that has its sway when all else fails;*
> *that wearies out all evil things;*
>   *that warms the depths of frozen fears*
> *making friend of foe;*
> *and lasts beyond the living and the dead,*
> *beyond the goals of peace, the ends of war!*
> *This we seek through all our years;*
> *to be complete and of one piece, within and without.[1]"*

There is no question that "to be of one piece without," as Thurman says, requires our attention to all of those systems which shape our lives as human beings. This is the work that so many of us have been engaged in for so long. It is crucial work. And in the face of so many urgent external threats in areas of health, the environment, economies, human rights, political instability, and regional and global aggression, it is understandable that our focus would be drawn to the world without, and that our work would involve conceiving instruments of peacebuilding that engage these issues and create the conditions for peace and human security.

But when we focus only on the instrumental mechanisms of peacebuilding, we fail to harness what may be the greatest power at our disposal to create cultures of peace, justice and healing. This power, as Dr. Thurman teaches us, emanates from the world within. It is a power flowing from the wholeness that is at the heart of humanity and indeed at the heart of life itself. It is the power of the human spirit. It is the feeling that we know when we hold a child in our arms, or are held by a beloved, or when we feel at home in the universe. It is love...and love's expressions: compassion, empathy, kindness, and generosity. It is the unbreakable bonds of human connection forged through the building of sustainable relationships. Let us then seek this through all our years as we contribute to building the beloved community among all the peoples of the planet.

Howard Thurman, For the Inward Journey: The Writings of Howard Thurman (New York: Harcourt Brace Jovanovich, 1984) p11

The Rev. Victor H. Kazanjian, Jr. Prior to joining URI as Executive Director in October 2013, Victor served as the dean of Intercultural Education and Religious and Spiritual Life, co-director of the Peace and Justice Studies Program, and director of the Peace Studies Program in India at Wellesley College, in Wellesley, Massachusetts USA. In addition he is the co-founder and co-president of Education as Transformation Inc., an international organization that works on issues of religious diversity and spirituality in higher education. Victor is also a visiting faculty member and Fulbright Scholar at the Malaviya Center for Peace Research at Banaras Hindu University in Varanasi, India, where he served as Fulbright Professor of Peace & Justice Studies. Victor's work at Wellesley College and through Education as Transformation is widely acknowledged as the catalyst in the national and international movement to include religion and spirituality as core issues in higher education, and has led to interfaith and intercultural growth and understanding. Specializing in inter–religious dialogue and conflict transformation, diversity and democracy, and peace building, Victor is a recognized thought leader and the author and editor of numerous books and articles. Victor Kazanjian is an ordained priest in the Episcopal Church and was trained as a community organizer working to address the systemic causes of poverty and injustice through the support of religious and community-based groups. He holds a Master of Divinity degree from the Episcopal Divinity School in Cambridge, Massachusetts, and is a graduate of Harvard University.

26

WHAT MOTHER MARY MEANS TO ME

By Afeefa Syeed

At Christmas time I hum along to the *Little Drummer Boy* song. I always wanted to be that drummer who gave a gift to the new born King and makes Mary smile. And I'm reminded again that the more I learn and reflect about the many manifestations of Mary, mother of Jesus, the more I am in awe of her.

Her story and place in history has been a source of strength for my soul and life, especially as a woman and as a mother. Although my understanding of Mary's story is based on the Quran's telling of her role - an entire chapter *Maryam*, is named after her - I've also gathered inspiration from women I've met, who interpret her story for their own lives. I've revisited her through various stages of my life and find ways that I might fill the gaps in how much we really know about someone who lived centuries ago.

The story starts with Hanna, Mary's mother who made a vow while pregnant, dedicating her unborn child to God for the benefit of humanity:

"Oh my Lord! I do dedicate unto You what is in my womb for thy special service. So accept this of me, for You hear and know all things." (Quran 3:35)

At that time, this dedication would mean sending the child to the temple to live, serve, and be raised. Besides a consecration to the physical temple, this conscious act of dedication reminds us as mothers-to-be that the collection of our thoughts, actions and mindfulness during pregnancy has bearing on our wombs and what develops within. We are not just vessels to carry a life into the world, but how we think about the child and how we treat our bodies can have consequences on the emotional, mental, and physical development of a fetus.

During each of my three pregnancies, I read Hanna's prayer and imbibed the notion that what I felt could be transferred to my unborn child. This moved me to write notes to each child somersaulting inside me, become more in tune with how my body was behaving and observe closely what each yet-to-be born little one was exposed to.

When Hanna's child was born and turned out to be a girl, she did not step away from her vow. She insisted that she had dedicated the *child* in her womb, not differentiating between a boy or girl. She is told that although the societal norm did not grant females such a ranking, God accepts her dedication. Hanna says:
"...I have named her Mary and I commend her and her offspring to Your protection from any Evil."...Right

graciously did her Lord accept her: He made her grow in purity and beauty." (3:36-37)

This is the basis for shattering double standards as a practice; that roles for benefit of society or in service of God can be performed by anyone dedicated to doing so. And this also speaks to the responsibility of each to assert this equality either for themselves or to advocate for others who cannot. Working in international development, I've heard Hanna's example resonate in various women's empowerment programs and efforts embedded with worldviews that respect and honor the role of Mary.

As she grows, Mary spends a great deal of time in a space in the temple called the *mihrab*, or niche. She passes her time praying and communing with a higher presence regularly, without intermediaries, she has direct connection and contact with the divine. But even more so I imagine her as a student and aspiring scholar who learns independently.

She must also have been cognizant of the temple's many dimensions of influence and power, which eventually will come to be seen as monopolizing of religious authority in that society. She chooses to separate from politics and social hierarchy and instead create a sanctuary and focus on bettering herself while considering solutions to what may be happening outside her sacred space.

Although she is to be the mother of Jesus, this is the span of time I realize that she herself has importance and value in how she made her own mark in society. To this day, that safe space Mary created for connectivity with God, the *mihrab*, is honored in mosques. In fact, it is also the spot from where community leaders deliver sermons, which should ideally uphold the call for justice and equality.

After it is revealed to her that she will carry a child, Mary submits to her destiny after hearing from Gabriel that it is the Creator's will. She has that unshakeable faith. However, when she goes into the throes of labor, she cries out:

"Ah! Would that I had died before this! Would that I had been a thing forgotten and out of sight!" (19-23)

She realizes that the responsibility of explaining her condition will be great and that the pain she endures is overwhelming. This plea from her reminds me that it is acceptable, even for someone who has received God's grace and blessings, to not only doubt herself, but wonder if what she is being called for is even possible physically, mentally or emotionally. Of course this well resonates with so many of us who, in the midst of labor, have shouted out all sorts of pleas and heartfelt cries!

In response to her cries of suffering through childbirth, Mary receives revelation telling her to hold fast to the trunk of a nearby palm tree as the pain crescendos and she is alone. She's told to eat dates and drink from the stream running nearby to keep her strength. This set of directives assures me that while prayer is powerful and important, solutions are linked to our own action and taking responsibility for our condition. Her pain could have been easily eliminated in response to her prayers, or not have even been necessary since she was under divine protection.

But to me, the lesson here is to understand what we can have control over, what is beneficial knowledge for us to have on hand, and how our actions can make a difference. In addition, for both men and women to understand that the experience of childbirth is grounded in the physical realm and needs to be recognized as a difficult process, in this case even for the mother Jesus. In fact, centuries later, Prophet Muhammad would equate the pains of labor with battles to fight injustice – the reward for dying during both are that of being a martyr in the cause of serving God.

Mary's role does not end with the birth of Jesus. She continues as a devout believer in the greater good and as a dedicated teacher who imparts on her growing son values of quiet empathy, recognizing imbalanced influences of power structures, and the persistent potency of prayer. Some 30 years of learning from his mother and this diligent upbringing, coupled with the Divine's destiny for him, Jesus becomes the Christ who himself teaches principles of equality and justice – to serve the poor and give voice to the oppressed.

He also came to confront and question the monopoly and hegemony of religious institutions that had taken access to God away from everyday people. He spoke truth to power that was masquerading as religious dogma and authority. In part, it has been argued that the reason Jesus was born without a father was to demonstrate to the religious leaders that their projection of being over protective fathers of the masses was misinformed and against divine precepts.

The Biblical and Quranic stories of Mary are especially moving to me, as I've interpreted them to see her as a fellow woman aspiring to spiritual connectivity, who creates her own space and place for understanding of all things Divine and worldly, and finally being able to impart these to others who, for her, included the Prophet of Peace, Jesus Christ.

As my sons grow into themselves and explore spiritual relationships on their own terms, Mary continues to teach me the value of sharing the practice of perseverance and patience. And even more, as I myself continue to evolve as a person, I realize that stories such as Mary's are much deeper and resonate more when we make them a part of our lives in practice, beyond being frozen on an unreachable pedestal.

Afeefa Syeed is a cultural anthropologist working in international development based in Washington, D.C., and the mother of three boys.

27

THE THIRD FIRE

Andrew Harvey

We all need to get into shape now. I think the most important thing is to understand the nature of the Divine. The nature of the Divine is both deeply peaceful and radically, dynamically active. The Hindu tradition expresses this as the marriage of Siva and Shakti, as the marriage of the peace and radiance of the diamond with the fiery light that diamond gives that creates everything.

What I call forth in my book *The Hope, A Guide to Sacred Activism*, is the road map for this fusion of radical, mystical knowledge, passion, and peace with clear wise focused action in the world. The clue to realizing this is to understand that God is both the great peace and the great passion. And, that we are called as children of God, to unite the two.

When I was trying to formulate my vision of sacred activism, there were two major initiations that happened to me that gave me the real insight. The first occurred when my father was dying in the place that I was born, in South India. There I had a vision of the Christ in church and what happened was that the statue of the Christ came alive! This huge force of the divine passion in the form of fire came from the statue and ripped open my heart. It woke up a volcano of Divine love in my own heart. My fire and the fire of the Christ, the fire of love itself, became an immense experience, one immense flame of passion.

I went out into the Indian streets and saw an armless and legless young man. I saw in his eyes the same Christ that I'd seen blazing in glory in the church. I heard this tremendously loud and ferocious voice saying, "You have been playing with the light, you have used it to decorate your ego and to go off into an addiction to transcendence, don't you realize the world is burning to death, animals are being destroyed, the habitat of the world is being destroyed, the environment is being destroyed, we're creating a death machine of injustice, craziness, and cruelty.

You've had the mystical experiences you've had not to go off into some private ecstasy, but to use the power and the fuel of those experiences to make yourself strong enough, vibrant enough, critical enough, clear enough, wise enough and passionate enough to start turning up in the world to do my work of justice and compassion." That was a huge wake up call for me, as you can imagine.

The second happened about a year later. I had another vision. In this vision, I saw two rivers of fire racing towards the horizon and when they met at the horizon they exploded together in a vast nuclear explosion. It wasn't a destructive explosion but a birth, a birth of a new wild, gorgeous all transforming force. As I witnessed this, I heard, "These two rivers are the two most powerful forces in the human soul, the fiery force of the mystic's passion for God, and the fiery force of the activist's passion for justice. When these two passions come together, when these two fires meet, a third fire is created. This third fire is the fire of love and wisdom in action. With this fire all things can be made new."

Chaos can become order. Apocalypse can become grace. Devastation can be healed. And, the paralysis and the narcissism of the human world, in its current terrifying manifestation, can be transformed into a humble alignment with the will of God, to transform all existing institutions, all ways of being and doing – everything, to create the kingdom on earth, the kingdom/queendom on earth.

That was a revelation. It was a huge, huge revelation; and, it's from that revelation that I've created the term *Sacred Activism* which really describes this fusion of the passion of the mystics God with the passion of the activists for justice.

The two most sensitive groups of people have been, in a way, collared and restrained by a subtle narcissism which can only be healed by incorporating the best of the other. So when the mystic really wakes up to the sacredness of the world, the sacredness of the animals, the sacredness of the environment, the sacredness of every human being and every sentient being and the enormous danger that we are in and the necessity to put love into action, the healing of the narcissism of the mystic takes place.

When the activist wakes up to the holiness of everything, the holiness of the essential enterprise of justice, the holiness of every being, the deep sacred identity of every being, then the whole enterprise of activism becomes grounded in a very much deeper spiritual power which actually helps the activist look after himself or herself, helps the activist to not burn out, gives the activist the courage and the patience to go on loving, and acting from the deepest possible place, not become defeated, discouraged, disappointed, and devastated by the inevitable difficulties of action.

So when the mystic's passion for God and the activist's passion for justice come together in a human being, what happens is that this elemental, primordial fire, this third fire is activated in that person and they become secret agents, if you like, of the evolution of the Divine. They become capable of transforming this chaotic planet into a place where Divine law, Divine harmony, Divine love reign and enable us to transform this apocalyptic situation we're in into a massive opportunity for a holy new way of being and doing everything.

For a long time we believed that we could in some way prevent what is about to unfold and what's already unfolding. That gave us great urgency and great passion and, sometimes, great rage. Now I think that we're all aware that the world is in terrible shape -the corporations, the governments, and the media are in absolute denial of what's truly going on and the great shattering, the collapse of all of our human agendas and faculties and of our current way of living in now certain.

When you first face the possibility of this terrifying collapse and become aware that it is going to be very difficult, very painful, and very dangerous, you can step back and really try and understand this chaos from a Divine perspective. You can see that it is actually what the mystics call the dark night. It is not a punishment. It is not a devastation that's going to lead to extinction. It is a process, very severe, through which human egotism, human fantasy of control, human fantasy of exploitation and domination of nature, are going to be systematically and ruthlessly destroyed. Not to destroy the human race, but to give it an extraordinary opportunity to humble itself, align itself with the divine will, and start working together beyond dogma, beyond racial and tribal separations, to create a unified humanity. A humanity dedicated to putting Divine love, Divine will, and Divine intelligence into radical action on every level of the world.

The dark night in the mystical traditions is known as this terrible ordeal though which the full self is unraveled, not as a punishment but as an opportunity to enter into the much more spacious, much more loving, much more compassionate Divine self – a great evolutionary crisis is going to happen. It's going to be very difficult but it is going to happen so those of us who see that the shattering is inevitable, who see that this is a mystery of transformation, are now preparing ourselves to put in place the structures that can shepherd humanity through this ordeal.

I think that one of the dangers of the new age has been its relentless concentration on the Divine as light itself. So there is a prevailing notion in the new age which is extremely dangerous that if you talk about environmental destruction; if you talk about the horror of two billion people living in poverty; if you talk about the devastating way we are treating animals; if you talk about the really horrific domination of the corporations and the bottom line mentality of everything that we do; if you talk about the paralysis that's pervading human society at the moment; you are in some way creating it, which is absurd. You've got to be able to analyze and face the radical illness that is threatening us at this moment and threatening the whole planet.

Shadow work is essential for the sacred activist and there are two kinds of shadow that need to be faced as deeply as possible, from as sacredly and profound a place as possible. First, is the collective shadow, we have to realize that we have created a death machine in our pathological belief in unlimited growth, in our pathological understanding of the human self as having absolute rights over animals, over nature, over the exploitation of animals and nature, and in our addiction to comfort and to a lifestyle which is ruining the earth. We also have to face the ways in which our own private shadow colludes with this collective shadow.

What I have done in my book, *The Hope* is to lay out what I believe the collective shadow is making us all feel at a sacred and deep level - which is very painful, but has to be faced. I think that there are five aspects of this collective shadow that every sacred activist will need:

1. Denial that anything terrible is going on while it's ravaging the earth;
2. Disbelief that we just can't believe that we are as destructive in our current consciousness as we are;
3. Deep dissolution at human nature during the 20th Century in which hundreds of millions of people died in war and genocide, and in which we allowed environmental catastrophes to flower while we all continued to embrace a consumerist culture;
4. Deep dread because as soon as you start to face all of this, you feel "oh my god, what are we going to have to go through?"; and
5. A great death wish because facing all of these things is overwhelming and people often say to me, "I just wish I wasn't here. Part of me wants to die. I want to get out of this horrific situation. I just don't think the human race is able to cope with it. The violence ahead is so terrible, the pain ahead is so terrible".

What I've discovered is that when you do really deep scared practice, when you ground yourself in God, then you can create a container large enough to make all of these five aspects of the collective shadow conscious in you and you won't be overwhelmed and destroyed by them. You become more deeply, calmly, urgently committed to doing the work of the transformation because you see just what is at stake if it isn't done.

Once you face the five collective shadows, you really do need to look at the ways in which your private shadows collaborate with this death machine. I think we're all addicted to comfort, we've all been spoiled and coddled by the consumerist culture, and this culture of unlimited growth. We're all terrified of really standing up to it because we all know how ruthless it can be to people who stand up to it. We're all wounded from our childhoods and from the sufferings that we've been through; and, we can use those wounds to hide behind and to feel impotent.

I think of what I call the golden shadow, which is what we project onto people like the Dalai Lama or Mother Theresa, a kind of glowing specialness which we feel we don't have; so, we worship them for what they do without claiming what they do as signs to us of what we can do.

The Dalai Lama has said to me, "I'm just an ordinary person. I've turned up. I do what I do. I do the sacred practices and people keep saying, "Oh you're so special.

I'm not special, I am you, I am somebody who is authentic."

What we have to face is that we all have this power of sanctity within us. This golden shadow that we indulge in, of projecting our own divinity onto others, is actually something that keeps us subtly imprisoned.

To come into your full power as a divine human being, as a sacred activist, you need to do and to continue to do massive shadow work on all the things that keep you embracing limitation, embracing despair, embracing comfort, embracing the current way of doing things and to really offer them up for transformation. This is very difficult work, but it can be done and it must be done by everybody and it must be done by us together.

There are two great advantages of doing this work. The first is that the old way of blaming and projecting your own stuff onto others ends, you really do have to face that it's not just the CEO's, the politicians, the heads of corporations, and the heads of media who are consumed by greed and self-importance and who are living lives of great carelessness - we all are doing the same thing to a certain extent. Sacred activism stops this kind of blaming and enables us to realize that we are part of this huge problem and therefore, we all have to do the work together.

The second thing that happens from this kind of shadow work is that because you've been brave enough

167

to identify the greed and the self-importance, the cowardice, the denial, the disbelief and the death wish in yourself, then you become much more compassionate and much more skillful in dealing with it in other people, and in helping other people to begin to face it and deal with it themselves.

Shadow work has an essential place because until you do this work, you're in la la land; and, we cannot afford to be in la la land at this moment, because any illusion about ourselves is dangerous now. The wonderful thing that you do discover of course when you do this profound shadow work and you go through many zones of despair and paralysis and sadness at humanity and at yourself, the extraordinary thing that you discover is that God is mercy; and that, when you make conscious this inner darkness and offer it up to the beloved for transformation, you are flooded by great love and great joy and great power and a great sense that you are not limited to this but that you become aware of this, go forward with a much deeper sense of purpose and a much more skillful humility.

One of the things that we do as spiritual friends and helpers and guides and teachers is to really give permission to people to feel the great grief they feel. It's so important to go through the heartbreak and I think that we live in a culture in which heart break and pain and suffering and deeply, deeply opening to the grief we feel are demonized, are dismissed as non-Divine or, even more, as ignorant. They're not ignorant, they're keys to connecting with the Divine heart.

I think there are three main things that all of us, who are doing this work of helping preparing the birth in this death, really need to get over to people. I think that we can do this in very simple and direct ways. The first thing is to stress to people the necessity of having a daily down home incessant spiritual practice. You're simply not going to be able to sustain the energy to do the work if you are not grounding every way, in every day your whole being in God.

There are four ways of spiritual practice that people need to get down now:
1. Cool practices that keep you calm in everything and these include the wonderful meditation practices, awareness practices, walking meditations, visualizations that calm you down, saying the name of God in your heart;
2. Heart practices that keep the heart alive and vibrant even in the most difficult situations. Heart practices that align yourself with the heart of the Divine;
3. Prayer practice as a way of keeping alive faith, and keeping alive connection to the Divine so that you can be guided even in the most extreme and difficult situations by the Divine intelligence, by the Divine will, by the Divine peace; and
4. Body practices. I think many people who are beginning don't understand the role of the body

in this great transformation. We need to bless the body, to sanctify the body, to look after the body and to dedicate the body to Divine transformation.

When you combine these four kinds of practices and shadow work then you are really, giving yourself the present of your own deepest human divinity; and, you'll be strong enough to do the work.

The second thing is to help people in their own localities start creating community. We cannot do this transformation alone. If we try to do it alone, we will very soon get discouraged, and feel isolated and helpless. We need to do it with other people. So I think to set up circles in which people can practice together, and mourn together is essential.

The third way is to say to people, "Now that we've come through and awakened a sense of where we are and what needs to be done, we need to realize that the reason goodwill, still present in humanity, isn't being more effective is because we are radically disorganized."

In these three things, I feel that we have the training for an army of lovers and servants of God to go out there and birth the birth in the real world.

Andrew Harvey is an author, religious scholar and teacher of mystic traditions, known primarily for his popular nonfiction books on spiritual or mystical themes, beginning with his 1983 A Journey in Ladakh. He is the author of over 30 books, including, The Hope, A Guide to Sacred Activism, The Direct Path, the critically acclaimed Way of Passion: A Celebration of Rumi, The Return of the Mother and Son of Man. He was the subject of the 1993 BBC documentary "The Making of a Modern Mystic" and is the founder of the Sacred Activism movement.

Harvey lives in a rural area of the Ozark Mountains in Arkansas, where he continues to write when he is not lecturing. Harvey conducts workshops on Sacred Activism, the teachings of Rumi, yoga, and practices that will lead to deeper spiritual awareness. Harvey travels with students to sacred sites in India, Australia, and South Africa, and offers personal spiritual direction.

28

CONCLUSION

I realized through the authoring of this book, *Awakening the Heart of the Beloved Community*, that I was awakening my heart; and, the more writers who came on board with their stories, the more I realized I was having an individualized experience with the Beloved Community. I realized that I am the Beloved Community: I am of African American, Native American, Irish American ancestry. I am a daughter, a mother, a grandmother, an auntie, a partner in a same gender loving relationship, and I am a mystic. I express myself through my service to humanity and Mother Earth as a peace walker and peace weaver of people and voices for the greater good. Having this awareness brought me face to face with the "inner me", and the "me in the world". I realized I had to learn to reconcile all of me, and find the peace within. I also realized that all of my differences make me the person I am today.

What a journey we have been on since you first opened the book, *Awakening the Heart of the Beloved Community*. Each of us, in our own words, have placed on the table our passion for peace, love, and transformation by opening our hearts to the reader.

Some chapters may have touched you more in the now. Others will rest in the back of your mind, working gently and subtly, until you are ready to grasp their full impact. Some chapters you may have found to be gentle and nurturing and some to be disturbing. Some will immediately inspire action and some will make you pause.

That is the way of the *Beloved Community*. It is the gift of our diversity that makes us stronger, that reminds us that we are in this world together. Diversity enables us to witness and engage the endless reflections of possibilities of the human being. Rich is our well of possibility when we release ourselves to a greater "wholeness".

We begin that process through self-awareness, truth telling, and deep listening; to connect with other-awareness and the deep work of merging the two: *me in others* and *others in me*.

ABOUT THE AUTHOR

Audri Scott Williams

The First Woman To Lead a Global Walk for Peace

Audri Scott Williams was the Vision Keeper who led the Trail of Dreams World Peace Walk over 6 continents (2005-2009), and the 13 Moon Walk 4 Peace across America to over 50 communities (2010-2011). She has received numerous awards for her service to humanity. Awards include: the Presidential Certificate of Merit (President Bill Clinton), HBO Hearing Her Voice, Telling Her Story Award; Volvo for Life American Heroes Award; and the 2008 URI Bowes Award to the Trail of Dreams Team (awarded in India). She holds a Masters in Liberal Arts from Naropa University/Creation Spirituality in Indigenous Science, a BA in Criminology from the University of Tampa, with post graduate studies at Harvard University, University of Maryland, and American University.

She is a woman of considerable intellectual and professional accomplishments. She served as the Interim Global Indigenous Coordinator for the United Religions Initiative (2013-2014) and co-convener of the Hidden Seeds Global Indigenous Gathering in Northern California (2014). She was an Apprentice with the WorldWide Indigenous Science Network (WISN), where she escorted and documented

175

indigenous wisdom keepers around the world; a former Dean of Instruction at the Institute of Divine Wisdom in Atlanta, Ga.; and Dean of Continuing Education and Community Service at Charles County Community College for over 8 years.

Audri, along with Jon Ware, Sr., co-founded a theatrical company, Uprising, in the performing arts in Washington D.C. She currently serves as a Trustee on the United Religions Initiative Global Council and is Co-founder, with Karen Hunter Watson, of the Quantum Leap Transformational Center. She has authored several books and produced documentaries about her journeys.

As a global peace walker and advocate for evolutionary change in the world, while advocating for a sustainable and viable world for generations to come, she is dedicated to the Beloved Community, and dedicates herself to the realization of the beloved community.